VARVARA STEPANOVA

Two Figures, 1920. Oil on plywood, 32 × 27.7.

VARVARA STEPANOVA
The Complete Work

ALEXANDER LAVRENTIEV
Edited by John E. Bowlt

The MIT PRESS
Cambridge, Massachusetts

Editorial conception: Passigli Progetti
Art Direction: Anthony Mathews

Design: Alexander Lavrentiev with Studio Branzi (Jim Obata)

Translated from the Russian by Wendy Salmond

All measurements are given in centimeters, height before width.

Endpapers: *front* Opening scene from *An Evening of the Book,* 1924;
back Intermission from *An Evening of the Book,* 1924.

First MIT Press Edition, 1988
© 1988 Idea Books Edizioni, Milan. Originally published in Italy
under the title *Varvara Stepanova, Una vita costruttivista.*

Set, printed and bound in Italy.

Library of Congress Cataloging-in-Publication Data

Lavrentiev, Alexander Nikolaevich.
    Varvara Stepanova, the complete work / Alexander Lavrentiev;
  edited and translated by John E. Bowlt. — 1st MIT Press ed.
      Bibliography: p. 188
      ISBN 0-262-12135-2
      1. Stepanova, Varvara Fedorovna, 1894-1958 — Criticism and
  interpretation. 2. Art — Themes, motives. I. Stepanova, Varvara
  Fedorovna, 1894-1958. II. Title.
N6999.S74L37   1988
709'. 2'4—dc 19   88-19145
                                                       CIP

CONTENTS

Portrait of Varvara Stepanova, 1932. Photo Alexander Rodchenko.

Varvara Stepanova, A Frenzied Artist

That is how the poet Vladimir Maiakovsky once described Varvara Fedorovna Stepanova (1894-1958), a prime mover of the Russian avant-garde and the subject of this monograph.[1] Stepanova did, indeed, live in a creative fury, never content with a single style, always experimenting with new concepts of painting, drawing, and design. She was in close contact with leading artists, poets, and film-makers of her time — Alexei Gan, Vasilii Kandinsky, Maiakovsky, Liubov Popova, Alexander Vesnin and, of course, her husband Alexander Rodchenko; she investigated an entire constellation of aesthetic tendencies — from *Jugendstil* to Constructivism, from Suprematism to Socialist Realism; and she supported the primary cultural institutions that determined the radical culture of early Soviet Russia — INKhUK (Institute of Artistic Culture), *LEF* (the magazine Left Front of the Arts), IZO NKP (Visual Arts Section of the People's Commissariat for Enlightenment), and VKhUTEMAS (Higher State Art-Technical Studios). Stepanova, then, was an essential contributor to, and product of, the "Great Experiment,"[2] and many of the outstanding achievements in stage, textile, and typographical design of the 1920s were the consequence of her theoretical elaborations and creative endeavors.

Stepanova was one of the "amazons of Russian art,"[3] and she is often mentioned alongside other women artists of her generation such as Natalia Goncharova, Valentina Kulagina, Popova, and Olga Rozanova. But like them, Stepanova tends to be connected too readily with her male companion (Rodchenko), a critical matchmaking that also integrates Goncharova with Mikhail Larionov, Kulagina with Gustav Klutsis, Popova with Vesnin, and Rozanova with Alexei Kruchenykh. Stepanova's marriage to Rodchenko was a successful union, producing not only a gifted child, the graphic artist and designer Varvara Rodchenko, but also many joint artistic ventures, especially in the sphere of book design. As her grandson, Alexander Lavrentiev, the author of this monograph and himself an artist, has noted, Stepanova and Rodchenko worked as a collective. Consequently, many of Stepanova's paintings and drawings bring to mind the concurrent work of Rodchenko (and vice versa), and, since they shared the same studio, materials, commissions, and friends, we should not be surprised at coincidences in form and content, whether in the visual poetry and collages of 1918-19, the linocut figures of 1919-20 or in the layouts for the propaganda albums of the 1930s. Even their respective self-portraits of 1920 seem to have been painted by the same hand. Of course, Stepanova paid homage to a variety of topical iconographic sources — from Henri Matisse (cf. his *Red Room* of 1908 with her painting of the same name of 1920) to Klutsis (cf. his political photomontages of the late 1920s with her compositions for the album *Itogi pervoi piatiletki* [Results of the First Five-Year Plan] of 1932). But Stepanova was master as well as apprentice, and her artistic psychology was different from Rodchenko's. She did not share his unbridled enthusiasm for abstract painting in spite of her advocacy of non-objective creativity in 1919;[4] she gave little attention to three-dimensional construc-

tions and architectural design; and she was not totally convinced of the uniqueness of photography, even though she did understand the prerogatives of the machine-made object vis-à-vis the hand-made one.

For the extrovert and sociable Stepanova, communication was the real justification of art. The raucous sounds of her visual poetry shout at us, her rhythmical figures invite us to dance, her posters and book illustrations convey the message loud and clear, her images of the railroad, the telephone, the radio, the movies express her fascination with mass communications. This is why Stephanova maintained that artistic construction should not be an end in itself and why in the early 1920s she adjusted so easily to utilitarian design. After all, the human face and figure — "robots," musicians, billiard-players, Charlie Chaplin, families — are recurrent motifs in her work. Building bridges between art and reality, therefore, was Stepanova's principal concern, and all the phases of her artistic career can be associated with this human relevance — with reaching out and speaking.

One of Stepanova's most remarkable inventions was her visual or, as she called it, graphic poetry of 1917-19 contained in her miniature syntheses of "non-objective" poems and images such as *Rtny khomle* and *Gaust chaba*. In some cases (e.g. *Gly-Gly*), she illustrated the *zaum* or transrational poetry of Kruchenykh; in others, she composed and illustrated her own *vers libre*. In combining sounds to form new words devoid of conventional meaning and, therefore, universally (in)comprehensible, Stepanova was expanding the linguistic concepts of the Futurists before her such as Konstantin Bolshakov, Velimir Khlebnikov, and Kruchenykh. The sounds that she arranged in syncopated patterns — "Afta yur inka/Nair prazi/Tavenio lirka/Taiuz fai" (*Rtny khomle*)[5] — are jazzy, harsh, lapidary, as if she wished to recapture the "original" utterance, the primal poem, like the baby's gibberish or the witch doctor's mumbo-jumbo. Pavel Filonov, Kazimir Malevich, Rozanova and other artists of the avant-garde also wrote *zaum* poetry, but none of them accompanied their verses with dynamic visual structures which, like Stepanova's stage sets for Vsevolod Meierkhold's *The Death of Tarelkin* (1922), act as colored counterpoints to these brusque phonemes. The result is an audacious optophonic synthesis of radical neologism and abstract painting, a formal stenography that a number of writers and musicians — Andrei Bely, Kruchenykh, Mikhail Matiushin, Artur Lourié — were also exploring. It is interesting to note the reference to Russia's most avant-garde composer, Nikolai Roslavets, in one of Stepanova's illustrations to *Gly-Gly*.[6]

Stepanova's visual poetry, like her stick figures of approximately the same period, may give the impression of informality and accident, but in fact she prepared and preceded her productions with careful theoretical deliberation. Her lectures and writings demonstrate a lively and enquiring mind that challenged established canons while proposing new and audacious ones. Her interpretation of Constructivism, her contribution to the famous INKhUK debate on composition ("centrifugal") and construction ("centripetal"), her unhesitating acceptance of functional design as the logical successor to studio art at the "5 × 5 = 25" exhibition in 1921, her ideas on the question of textile and fashion design, her expansion of Gan's analysis of facture and tectonics — Stepanova's statements followed the same rationality and consistency that helped her create successful scenographic experiments, fabrics and costumes, and, above all, poster, book, and magazine designs.[7]

Stepanova's visualization of new sound and graphic patterns is a concern that enables us better to understand her concentration on the very media in which she excelled, stage, polygraphical, and textile design, for they all relate to the discipline of language (spoken, written, and gestural). Her commercial advertisements, book marks, and didactic posters of the 1920s are "objective" poems, simple, vivid, and accessible, even to the semi-literate — except in those few cases where typographical stylization makes letters unrecognizable (e.g. her cover for the book *Spetsializatsiia poezdov* [Specialization of Trains] of 1925. Even the sophisticated *Samozveri* [Autoanimals] of 1926 (a Stepanova-Rodchenko collaboration) and the intricate photomontages for the journal *USSR under Construction* in the 1930s, involving statistics, slogans, and excerpts from Stalin's speeches, can still be regarded as basic experiments in linguistic manipulation and graphic poetry.

Stepanova's attention to book design relates directly to her perception of the new social structure and its new human beings, streamlined, efficacious, economical, that El Lissitzky, Malevich, and Rodchenko also identified with the coming of Socialism. Indeed, Stepanova obviously intended her sets and costumes in Meierkhold's production of *The Death of Tarelkin* for some advanced industrial community inhabited by mechanical people whose geometric uniforms and minimal accessories facilitated their taylorized movements. The same is true of Stepanova's other experiments for the stage, *Through Red and White Spectacles* (1923) and the *Evening of the Book* (1924), and the movie *Alienation* (1926), in which she investigated the principles of "universality" and "standardization." Implementing the Constructivists' call for maximum effect through economy of means, Stepanova stood in complete antithesis to the *fin de siècle* designers who, as one critic mentioned, "had wrapped up the actor like candy in a pretty piece of paper."[8] Stepanova unwrapped him, restoring the sense of the *Körpergefühl* and placing her costumes among her "spatial objects" on stage.[9] In her scenographic resolutions, therefore, the stage became a truly architectural, three-dimensional experience.

Standardization and rationalization are terms that Stepanova also used in her formulation of new principles of fabric and dress design in 1922-24, particularly in her establishment of stereotypical or productional clothing — the so-called *prozodezhda*. Like Popova, Stepanova maintained that every profession (factory worker, teacher, actor, sportsman, doctor, etc.) needed its own uniform or costume which should be made in accordance with the standards of expediency dictated by that profession. The most dynamic example of Stepanova's experiments in this field were her projects for *sportodezhda* (sports clothes) dependent on bright colors (for easy recognizability) and lightness of material (for regulating body temperature). Unfortunately, her special clothing was not mass produced, although some of her fabric designs were simple, geometric, rhythmical, thanks to her brief tenure at the First Textile Printing Factory in 1923-24. Although she soon came to concentrate almost exclusively on books and magazines, Stepanova never lost interest in clothes design, and as late as 1929 published an article in connection with the Moscow "Exhibition of Everyday Soviet Textiles."

A woman of liberal compassion and democratic kindness, Stepanova must have found it difficult to adjust to the social and cultural strictures of the Stalin era. Certainly, with Rodchenko, Stepanova supported the political commitment of art and design in the 1930s, but she was, after all, a creative individual with a distinctive worldview that could not always be accommodated by the raw ideological dictates of that time. Perhaps that is why, like Rodchenko and Vladimir Tatlin, she turned back to a figurative, expressive manner of painting in the late 1930s, using her brush with the frenzy of her avant-garde years. As we look at Rodchenko's numerous photographs of Stepanova, we realize that she was an activist — a gifted actor — who, while retaining her original personality, never ceased to participate in the collective establishment of the new creativity that she identified with the "dawning of a great new epoch."[10]

John E. Bowlt

Notes

1. Maiakovsky wrote the following dedication on one of the books that he gave to Stepanova in 1923: "To the frenzied Stepanova with tenderest wishes. V. Maiakovsky." See illustration on p. 10.

2. A reference to Camilla Gray's early and still valuable study of the Russian avant-garde, *The Great Experiment. Russian Art 1863-1922* (London: Thames and Hudson, 1962), republished with revisions by Marian Burleigh-Motley as *The Russian Experiment in Art 1863-1922* (London: Thames and Hudson, 1986).

3. B. Livshits: *Polutoraglazyi strelets* (Leningrad: Izdatelstvo pisatelei, 1933), p. 143.

4. V. Stepanova: "Bespredmetnoe tvorchestvo" in catalog of "X Gosudarstvennaia vystavka: Bespredmetnoe tvorchestvo i suprematizm," (Moscow), 1919. The translation of this article appears in the text below.

5. See the page from *Rtny khomle* (1918) reproduced on p. 21.

6. See illustration on p. 29. Roslavets was a member of Malevich's Supremus group.

7. Translations of Stepanova's statements on art are included in the text below.

8. A. Ivanov: "Teatralnyi kostium" in E. Gollerbakh (ed.): *Teatralno-dekoratsionnoe iskusstvo v SSSR 1917-1927* (Leningrad: Komitet vystavki teatralno-dekoratsionnogo iskusstva, 1927), p. 157.

9. [A. Gan]: "Beseda s V.F. Stepanovoi" in *Zrelishcha* (Moscow), 16 (1922), 12-18 December, p. 11.

10. Stepanova, "Bespredmetnoe tvorchestvo," op. cit.

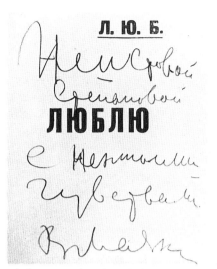

Vladimir Maiakovsky's dedication to Stepanova, 1923.

Display of Stepanova's works at the exhibition "Art and the Revolution. Part II," Seibu Museum, Tokyo, 1987.

Stepanova in her studio, 1924. Photo Alexander Rodchenko.

"To the frenzied Stepanova with tenderest wishes," wrote Vladimir Maiakovsky in his book *I Love* [Liubliu], published by the VKhUTEMAS press in 1922. Why the frenzied Stepanova? In coining this phrase Maiakovsky was defining Varvara Stepanova's temperament as a painter, but he was also emphasizing her strong adherence to principle in arguments about literature and art. And arguments and discussions there were. This explains why Maiakovsky inscribed another of his books, *War and Peace* [Voina i mir]: "To comrade Stepanova in memory of the attack on Friche. V. Maiakovsky. 4. III. 1922." (V. M. Friche (1870-1929) was a critic and historian of art and literature.) The reference here is possibly to one of the discussions that took place after Maiakovsky's poetry recital in the hall of the Polytechnic Museum. The words "with tenderest wishes" are more easily explained: Maiakovsky always treated his friends and sympathizers with consideration and affection. Alexander Rodchenko and Stepanova were both.

Rodchenko and Stepanova were more than just husband and wife. Together they formed a small creative unit, in which both members took part in many communal projects, and also worked independently. Rodckenko is the more famous, as a result of the greater number of publications and exhibitions devoted to him. Stepanova is known for her theater costumes and textile designs, but the rest of her oeuvre has yet to be discovered.

Varvara Stepanova was one of a group of extraordinary women artists who, no less than their male colleagues, laid the foundations of Soviet artistic culture. Some of them, like Natalia Goncharova, Olga Rozanova, and Nadezhda Udaltsova, have gone down in the history of art as painters. Others, for example Natalia Lamanova, are better known as fashion designers, those working primarily in decorative and applied art. Still others, like Alexandra Exter and Liubov Popova, cannot be categorized only as painters, or graphic artists, or theater or fashion designers. They are multifaceted individuals, and it is to this third group that Varvara Stepanova belongs. Over the past few decades her works have been shown at the exhibitions "Moscow-Paris," "Women Artists of the Russian Avant-garde," and "From Painting to Design" in Cologne, "Art into Production" at Oxford, and lastly at the joint monographic exhibition "Rodchenko and Stepanova" which toured West Germany, Italy and Czechoslovakia. In 1987 her works aroused a good deal of interest at the exhibition "Art and Revolution. Part II," held at the Seibu Museum in Tokyo. Stepanova's ideas have been adopted by fashion and textile designers and modern typographers like R. Napier and David King. Op-art has come back into fashion. Naturally these evaluations of Stepanova's work reflect the perspective of contemporary design in the 1960s to the 1980s, but there is yet another scale of values independent of the state of the market, an absolute scale on which to measure the innovations and originality of Stepanova's work.

First of all, Stepanova was an artist with a clearly defined "signature." The early works of Rodchenko and Stepanova left their mark, not only on the formation of early Constructivism, but also on the visual culture of the 1920s as a whole. Second, her easel paintings, experimental projects, and "production" works have an absolute novelty that can be seen in the geometric-figurative style of her painting, her concept of "visual poetry," her ideas for creating functional clothing, and her methods of graphic design. At the same time Stepanova was one of the first theorists of Constructivism. In her notes and articles on art she expounded interesting ideas on the specifics of artistic creativity, and the artist's place in industry. A third important reason for publishing Stepanova's oeuvre, therefore, is to allow her to speak for herself, to acquaint the reader with her own assessments of the artistic process.

In addition to her work as an artist and designer, Stepanova was also involved in academic and organizational activities. She took part in scholarly discussions and presented lectures, she recorded debates between members of INKhUK [The Institute of Artistic Culture] and transcribed Rodchenko's ideas, she taught at the Academy of Social Education and at VKhUTEMAS [Higher State Art-Technical Studios]. All these things point not only to Stepanova's distinctive personal destiny, but

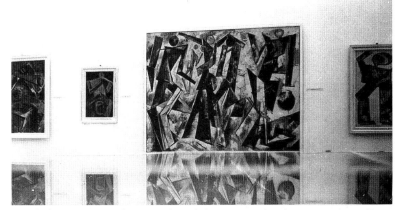

Works by Stepanova shown at the exhibition "Rodcenko-Stepanova. Alle origini del Costruttivismo," Palazzo Brasci, Rome, 1984.

Clothing designed by Stepanova shown at the exhibition "Moscow-Paris. 1900-1930," Moscow, 1982.

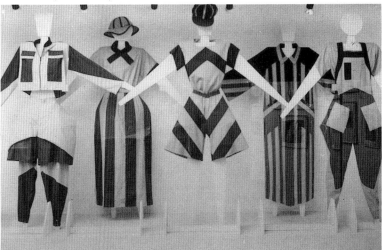

Figure with a Trumpet, 1920. Oil on canvas, 70 × 57.

also to her total participation in the artistic process of the 20s and 30s.

Varvara Stepanova's niece, the journalist and writer S. G. Stepanova, recalls that it was in the gymnasium school at Kovno (Kaunas) that the future artist's talents first appeared. The only things which have survived from this period are a silk bookmark decorated with roses, and a group photograph of the family. In order to be accepted as a student at the Kazan Art School, she was obliged to enter a fictitious marriage with an architect called Fedorov (he was later killed in 1914 during the war). It was at the school in 1913 that she met Rodchenko. From this time on, whenever she filled out the "area of specialization" section in questionnaires she would always write "artist-painter and lecturer on art."

Without completing her courses at Kovno she left for Moscow, the center of artistic life. For her, as for Rodchenko, it was important to make contact with others who shared her views. Stepanova studied painting in the studios of Konstantin Yuon and M. Leblanc, where she met, among others, Liubov Popova, Olga Rozanova, Vladimir Tatlin, Nadezhda Udaltsova, and Alexander Vesnin. Naturally, there was no money to be made from studying painting, and to earn a living she worked as a book-keeper in a factory and learned to type.

Stepanova, 1916, Moscow.

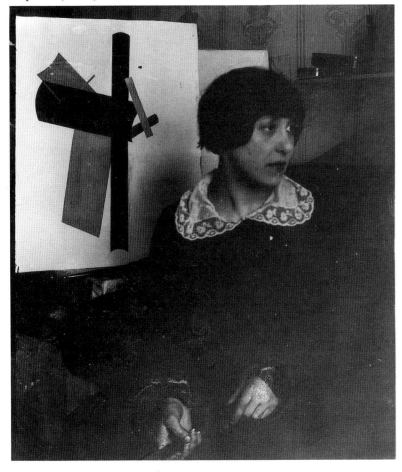

Mother and Child, 1919. Linocut.

Before this, however, she had bought herself a Singer sewing machine while working as a seamstress, and had acquired her knowledge of dress design while still at the Kazan Art School.

Stepanova, 1912, Kaunas.

Stepanova, her brother G. F. Stepanov, her mother A. I. Stepanova, the architect D. Fedorov (then Stepanova's husband), and her sister Z. F. Stepanova, c. 1913.

Even at this early date it is difficult to differentiate her fate, her dreams, and her hopes from those of Alexander Rodchenko. Life was still unsettled, the couple lived in different cities and saw each other only periodically. Constant communication therefore could only be through letters and poems dedicated to each other. The little exercise books in their oilskin bindings and the small envelopes are not like ours today. Rodchenko and Stepanova kept them through all their moves from city to city, from one apartment to another.

The envelopes travelled from Kazan, where Rodchenko still lived, to Moscow and back again. Stepanova would visit relatives in Kostroma, and Rodchenko would send letters to her at this new address. In their letters they would think up new and tender names for each other; there they were transported to a new and magical world of poetry, where Rodchenko was "King Leander the Fiery" and Stepanova "Queen Naguatta." This world of poetry was far better ordered than the real world, which only rarely surfaced in Stepanova's letters in the form of information about a new job or complaints about fatigue, trying times in the studio or success and new acquaintances. . . . But "the King" was far away, and so the Queen would write:

And today I put on a black dress
The black dress of my sorrow.

One can imagine these letters and words brought to life on the stage, and picture the two heroes of this play without an end. Rodchenko wrote:

Let it flow languorously through the strange halls
Slipping into a revery, sliding like a dream
My old fashioned waltz, my intoxicating waltz
My waltz woven of pale roses

My enemies are laughable, lurking behind masks
Hissing like snakes, hiding a dagger
But I am careless, concealing a bracelet
Holding a goblet in singing fingers

The goblet is poisoned, but the poison is vengeance . . .
The heart laughs . . . The clown is cunning . . .
But Columbine plays with passion
Pierrot chuckles . . . The clown trembles

Two Figures, 1912. Oil on canvas, 22 × 16.

Stepanova with students of the Kazan Art School, 1912.

Caricature of Stepanova, 1913. Drawing by Moshchevitin, a student at the Kazan Art School.

Let the heart ache . . . But the halls are strange
And the sea of revenge trembles in flowers
But I throw my bracelets in his face
And in reveries of a waltz drink the goblet . . .

To this Stepanova replied:

I saw you as the king of an immense kingdom, where your desires smouldered in the abyss. And it seemed to me that I do not know the whole secret of your soul. And I never will. You lift a corner of the curtain from the stars where your soul hides. I tremble and it comes to me that already I know much, but not the real thing . . . A new mystery is born . . . And I am once again disappointed . . . .

O Pierrot mine, powdered and pale
You mockingly slide through the splendid halls
Like a pale ray of silvery moonlight
Cold and haughty in the dark clouds
You lure everything to you like a terrible force
And weave cunning designs with Satan

You are mysterious to the core, elusive
Like the reflection from a dead opal
In a deep mirror of water . . .
And your weary glance is inscrutable
Like the cover of black night
Before the break of dawn

As early as 1913 Stepanova could sense the distinguishing features of Rodchenko's art: her poems are variations on the themes of Rodchenko's early graphic compositions, where the color black is present as a symbol of mystery and experiment, in which a strong element of analysis is evident.

Later, in 1915-16, Stepanova carefully copied the poems into a book made of thick paper with a velvety finish. The binding was of leather and fabric decorated in the Art Nouveau style. The binding material, the expensive Whatman paper, wide margins, delicate pen-drawn vignettes and illuminations, the letters with their little flourishes, were all intended to create the impression of an old, almost medieval handwritten book of sonnets, written in the spirit of Romantic Symbolism. The style of the illustrations reveals Stepanova's familiarity with the graphics of Aubrey Beardsley. On one page is a portrait of the King (easily recognized from the poems) done in the same manner. On the other the Queen is shown wearing a mask.

One of the first Moscow exhibitions in which Stepanova took part was "Decorative Artists in Aid of the Wounded," held at the Lemercier Gallery in 1916. Judging by the catalog, Stepanova exhibited two works, both entitled *Panneau*, and as far as we can tell the works sold, although their present whereabouts is unknown. One might speculate that they were somehow analogous to the only composition from this period that has survived, *Two Figures*. It depicts two women in magnificent gowns, the bright brush strokes of pure color imitating the splendour of their adornments and the play of the fabrics.

Visions of a Queen, 1914. Ink on paper, 9.8 × 9.7.

Visions of a Queen, 1914. Ink on paper, 6 × 6.

Figure, 1912. Oil on canvas, 25 × 15.7.

The democratization of public life ushered in by the 1905 Revolution and then by the October Revolution of 1917 had an immediate impact on the art world. The material position of young artists, deprived of steady jobs and commissions, had been no better than that of factory workers. To protect their interests and to be able to exhibit their works and rent studios, the artists formed their own union as early as 1917 — the Moscow Union of Painters. Together with IZO NKP [the Visual Arts Section of the People's Commissariat for Enlightenment], this union played an important role, advertising competitions for decorating the city during the revolutionary festivals, and implementing the plans for these spectacles. Three federations were created within the union — Senior, Middle, and Junior. Naturally, Rodchenko and Stepanova were members of the Junior Federation. Its president was Vladimir Tatlin, and Rodchenko was secretary.

During the period 1917-18 the old imperial bourgeois organizations collapsed. The system of art education was reformed, and Moscow's art institutes were changed into the State Free Art Studios, and exhibition politics were handled by the Union and IZO NKP. In 1918 the First and Second Exhibitions of paintings by the Union of Painters opened at the Art Salon, and among the 180 artists who took part were Stepanova and Rodchenko. Stepanova exhibited collage caricatures of artists (Ivan Kliun, Malevich, Popova, and Rozanova), and a new series of linocuts with expressiva figurative compositions. The State Exhibitions of Painting also began in 1918, in addition to the usual museum exhibitions and shows by groups formed before the Revolution ("The Knave of Diamonds," "The World of Art," "The Association of Travelling Exhibitions" ["The Wanderers"]). Stepanova's name first appears in the catalog of a State exhibition as a new member of the experimental-analytical trend in art. In addition to the painted landscapes, portraits, still lifes and wooden sculptures that were shown, the exhibition also included works that were rather out of the ordinary: compositions by Vasily Kandinsky from 1913 to 1917, reliefs constructed of different materials by Kliun, Alexander Rodchenko's "non-objective compositions of projected and colored planes," and finally display boards with graphic works arranged in series by Stepanova. They figure in the exhibition catalog as "four colored graphic works from the book *Rtny khomle*." For the first time in art exhibition history, works of a genre known as visual poetry were shown.

This was not a chance phenomenon. The art of the 1910s and 1920s had already intensified artistic experimentation. At one time, during 1914 to 1916, Tatlin's counter-reliefs or Bruni's assemblages had been totally innovative. The demonstration of this or that new art concept at an exhibition, whether as a work of art or a manifesto, guaranteed the author's prior claim to the new trend: Malevich "patented" the square and Suprematism; in 1919-20 Rodchenko "patented" the line and spatial construction by presenting an entire lecture on the subject; Stepanova promulgated the principle of "color-painted graphics." The years from 1918 to 1921 were extremely intense for the group of artists to which Rodchenko and Stepanova belonged, and there was a lot of joking and banter about competing for the acquisition of "isms." One avenue of inquiry concerned the process whereby a work of art becomes increasingly universalized and abstracted into a general formal and creative principle. "The picture is transformed into an experiment and a piece of scientific data," Stepanova later wrote. Or: "The picture is a formula for spatial construction." A process of maximum reduction in depictive information took place, like the collapse of a "black hole" that would later explode as the "supernova" star of a new style.

Cover design for *Gaust chaba*,
1918. Collage on paper,
27.5 × 17.

Illustrations for *Gaust chaba*, 1918. Ink on newspaper, 27.5 × 17.

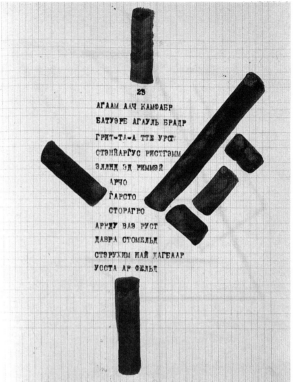

Varst (non-objective poems), 1918-19. Exercise-book cover.

Varst (non-objective poems), 1918-19. Pages from an exercise-book. Typewriting, ink and colored pencil, 23 × 18.5.

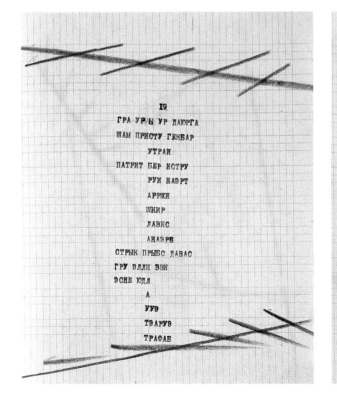

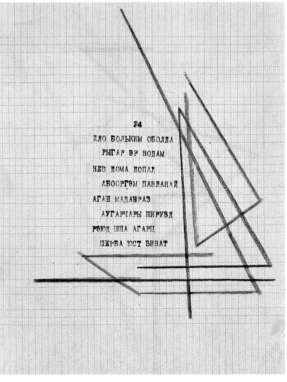

Cover for *Rtny khomle*, 1918. Tempera on paper, 23.5 × 17.7.

In Stepanova's graphic works of non-objective poetry, the extra-verbal communication is merged with the extra-objective form. On the one hand we see an abstract graphic composition, on the other a melodic reassembling of sounds that are just as conventional as the graphic form and color.

When Stepanova returned to poetry in the late 1910s her work was no longer Symbolist and Romantic, but rather an investigation of verbal and aural material in order to capture the consistency of our perception of individual sound combinations. An enormous stimulus for Stepanova in this research was the work of Olga Rozanova, who in 1916-17 had also written non-objective poems, trying various combinations of vowels and consonants to attain an expressive facture or texture of sounds, and to convey mood through what might be called palpable words. Rozanova conceived the development of non-objective poetry as still being within the genre of literature, in much the same way as her husband, the poet Alexei Kruchenykh, did. His famous "Dyr bul shchyl," one of the few poems in the world that needs no translation, was published in the miscellany *The Word as Such* [Slovo kak takovoe] in 1913 using conventional type-setting. In designing the lithographed books of Kruchenykh and Velimir Khlebnikov, Rozanova worked in a deliberately clumsy and crude graphic manner. Handwritten letters leaped and cavorted beside the drawing. In the books *Explodity* [Vzorval], *A Game in Hell* [Igra v adu] and others, the illustrations and the text interpenetrate.

Another area of investigation was the reconstruction of the book as an actual organism. Vasilii Kamensky and Ilia Zdanevich assembled the text from differently sized type cases — letters, vignettes, solids, even poster-size print. In his book *Ferroconcrete Poems* [Zhelezobetonnye poemy] Kamensky used wallpapers as the background for his compositions of typefaces on the page. Kruchenykh resorted to a variety of printing techniques unusual in book design — hectographs, linocuts, collage, lithography — for other reasons. First, he wanted to shock the "refined" literary public who were used to the luxurious publications of the Symbolists. Second, as a poet he wanted to have his words published as quickly as possible, no matter if the edition was small and the illustrations hand-done in watercolor. Rodchenko and Stepanova were familiar with many Futurist publications. Some of them they especially cherished — for instance, the first editions of Maiakovsky's early poems. What Stepanova did in her series was to transform visual poetry into a new, independent form of visual creativity, on a par with painting, graphics and sculpture. She demonstrated the concept of visual poetry by dividing the book into separate pages and attaching them to display boards. Moreover, she showed not one but several series, unified by the title of the book, its poetic structure, and the way the letters and shapes were presented.

The novelty of Stepanova's method lies in her attempt to unify the text's sound facture with its visual facture. The sound of a poem may be rough like a rough, natural material ("Shukh taz khkon"), smooth-flowing like a breath of wind

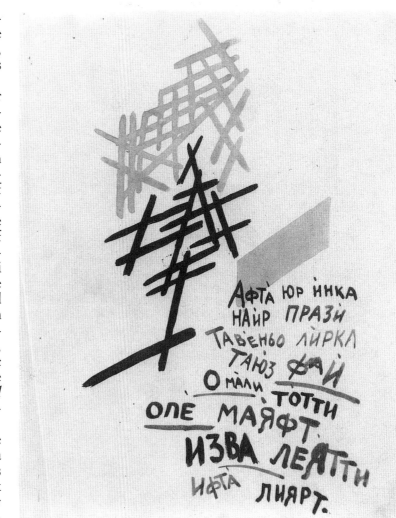

Illustration for *Rtny khomle*, 1918. Tempera on paper, 23.5 × 17.7.

"Fianta chiol"), or impulsive ("Afta iur inka"). These moods are graphically conveyed by the nature of the forms. The way a poem is written conveys the timbre and specific speed of speech. The apparent sound of the graphics that appears in the process of visual perception gives them a sense of duration and temporal development. The graphic component thus acquires the elements of time and movement, which was then a new means of expression. Color plays a major role in Stepanova's work. One might even speak of the text's color-facture. Color may be cool and recede deep into the page, or bright and warm, pulling off the surface of the page. Cool shades are in constant conflict with warm ones, just as in Stepanova's poetry vowels and consonants are in conflict:

I connect the new movement of non-objective poetry as sound and letters with painterly perception, and this imbues the sound of poetry with a new and vital visual impression. By turning the monotony of printed letters upside-down and fusing them with painterly graphics, I am approaching a new type of creativity.

Illustration for *Rtny khomle*, 1918. Tempera on paper, 23.5 × 17.7.

Illustration for *Rtny khomle*, 1918. Tempera on paper, 23.5 × 17.7.

On the other hand, by using painterly graphics to reproduce the non-objective poetry of the two books *A Game in Hell* and *Rtny khomle*, I am introducing the graphics of sound as a new quality into painting, thereby augmenting the quantitative possibilities of my graphic art.

Such was Stepanova's programmatic concept of these works, first published in the catalog to the 10th State Exhibition under the title "Non-objective Creativity and Suprematism." In addition to visual poetry, linocuts, and painting which depicted schematic human figures, Stepanova also exhibited a series of slogans, the texts of which were taken in part from the newspaper *Art of the Commune* [Iskusstvo kommuny]: "The future is our only goal;" "The proletariat is the creator of the future, not the heir to the past;" "Build the avant-garde of revolutionary proletarian art;" "Comrades, take up your hammers to forge the new word!" The slogans were handwritten and consisted of geometric forms, patches of color and inscriptions. Breaks in intonation and stress were reproduced graphically through variations in scale, color and form. The overall invocatory nature of the text was expressed through its abstract geometric construction.

Stepanova's experiments of 1919 are part of her wish to create a new image of the book. Sometimes she uses newspaper as a ground on which to print her poems. Pages with boldly written letters across a newspaper text alternate with collages composed of scraps of photographs and colored postcards. Elsewhere the poem is typewritten. In Stepanova's hands the typewriter — a writer's instrument — becomes a tool for the graphic artist. She looks for the form of a poem on the space of the page. Words are assembled to form triangles, rectangles, or two triangles one on top of the other. Rodchenko adds a few lines using colored pencils and a ruler, and the composition is finished.

Illustration for *Rtny khomle*, 1918. Tempera on paper, 23.5 × 17.7.

Composition, 1919. Linocut.

Figure, 1919. Linocut.

Reclining Figure, 1919. Linocut.

Composition, 1919. Linocut.

Composition, 1919. Linocut.

Varst, 1919. (The author's monogram.) Linocut.

Cover for *Globolkim*, 1918. Tempera on paper, 18.5 × 16.

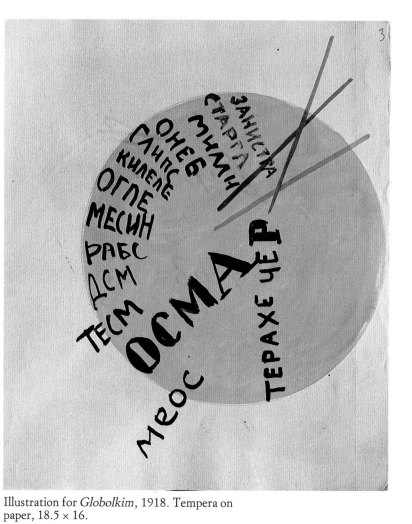

Illustration for *Globolkim*, 1918. Tempera on paper, 18.5 × 16.

Cover design for *Zigra ar*, 1918. Tempera on paper, 18.5 × 16.

Illustration for *Zigra ar*, 1918. Tempera on paper, 18.5 × 16.

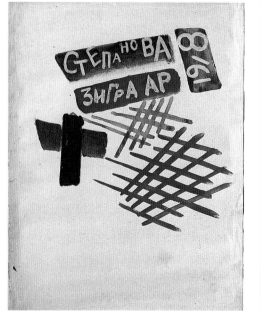

Illustration for *Zigra ar*, 1918. Tempera on paper, 18.5 × 16.

Illustration for Alexei Kruchenykh's *Gly-Gly*, 1919. Ink on paper, 15.5 × 11.

Illustration for Kruchenykh's *Gly-Gly*, 1919. "Olga Rozanova Dancing." Collage on paper, 15.5 × 11.

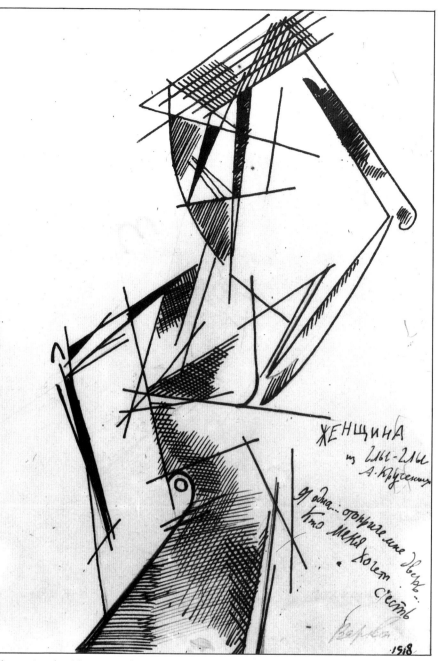

Illustration for Alexei Kruchenykh's *Gly-Gly*, 1919. Ink on paper, 15.5 × 11.

Illustrations for Kruchenykh's *Gly-Gly*, 1919. Ink and collage on paper, 15.5 × 11.

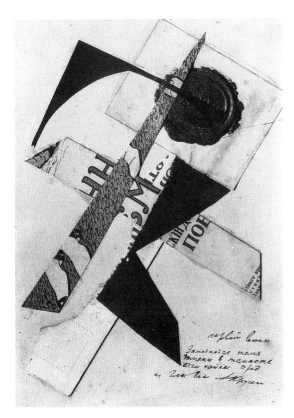

Handwritten poster: "Comrades, take up your hammers to forge the new world," 1919. Tempera on paper, 35.5 × 22.5.

Handwritten poster: "The proletariat is the creator of the future, not the heir to the past," 1919. Collage and white lead on paper, 35 × 22.5.

Handwritten poster: "RSFSR. The future is our only goal," 1919. Tempera on paper, 26.5 × 22.5.

Stepanova's works in the studio she shared with Rodchenko, 1921.

Wandering Musicians, 1921. The first double portrait of Rodchenko and Stepanova. The artists are depicted as if they were an animated painting composed of figures, geometric forms and a variety of materials.

Self-portrait, 1920. Oil on plywood, 71 × 52.

Musicians, 1920. Oil on canvas, 107 × 142.

Figure at the Easel, 1920. Tempera on paper, 40 × 35.

Two Figures at a Table, 1920. Gouache and ink on colored paper, 25 × 30.

Two Figures at a Table, 1920. Tempera on paper, 35 × 40. The entire image is constructed using tools "untouched by humand hands:" a paper stencil and an even, "mechanical" coloring of the surface using a half-dry bristle brush. Technique and style both create the image of a unified world where the forms of the human body, the furniture, and the picture on the wall are governed by the same general constructive laws.

Two Figures with a Ball, 1920.
Tempera on paper, 40 × 35.

Head, 1920. Ink and gouache on paper, 35.5 × 22.

Figure at the Easel. The Painter, 1920. Tempera on paper, 40 × 35.

Figure, 1920. Oil on canvas, 66 × 39.

Figure with a Trumpet, 1920. Tempera on paper, 40 × 35.

Two Figures, 1920. Linocut.

Seated Figure, 1920. Linocut.

Figure, 1919. Oil on canvas, 54 × 35.

Man Playing the Drum, 1920. Oil on cardboard. 44 × 31.

Stepanova's first works in the new *Figures* series date from 1919. At first they took the form of sketchy and very expressionistic linocut compositions. The figures flew upwards, danced and leapt. The move toward the schematization of the human figure can be seen in those sketches that survive from the early 20s. If the models in Liubov Popova's grandiose canvases were the result of her generalized, Cubist treatment of real space and form, then Stepanova's *Figures* had quite another source, that of ornamental graphics and decorative art. For her it was not so much a question of reduction as of construction, of an increasingly geometric modeling. *Figures* are an expression of the most general conception of man, an almost philosophical conception. Stepanova investigated and demonstrated typical poses: sitting, standing, dancing, jumping, talking. The area around the figures was composed of the same elements, though larger in scale. *Figures* embodied a particular view of the world, based on geometry, structure and order. Only one step separated these compositions from her new conception of clothing and geometric fabric designs.

Stepanova's *Figures* occur in both her painting and her graphic work. The same subject is rarely repeated twice. An exception is *Figure with a Trumpet*, although the tonal and color qualities in the graphic work are quite unlike those in the corresponding painting. Only the structure, the reciprocal arrangement of representational elements, is the same. The extensive graphic "Figures" series is unified by size, technique, and a common, almost square, format. Here Stepanova uses almost exclusively bright, saturated colors and what might be called non-artistic tools. There is almost no visible trace of brush or pencil; instead the whole is dominated by a velvety surface produced by applying paint over a stencil plate. The customary hand craft has been replaced by a sign or symbol of the machine-made, a mechanical facture. One tool Stepanova uses is a serrated wheel dipped in paint which produces lines of varying lengths made up of metrically spaced sections, dots, and divisions.

The first two to see Stepanova's "figures" were Robert Falk and Kandinsky, who were then living in the same building as Rodchenko and Stepanova. Rodchenko and Stepanova wanted to test the artists' reactions to this new series, and so gain some idea of how many they should exhibit, and where. Falk was overwhelmed by the abundance of the drawings, by their richness and freshness. He noted that Stepanova's temperament produced works quite distinct from Rodchenko's calmly rational ones. The experiment proved successful, and an expanded series of paintings and graphic works on this theme was shown, first at the 19th State Exhibition in 1920, then later at the Exhibition of Four Artists.

Men Playing Billiards, 1920 (no. 14). Oil on canvas, 66 × 129.

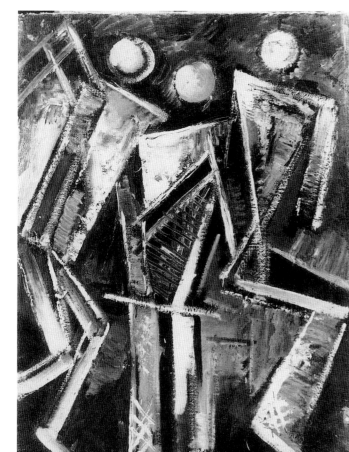

Three Figures, 1920 (no. 28). Oil on plywood, 70.5 × 52.5.

The Red Room, 1920. Oil on canvas, 62 × 53.

Among the works exhibited were *Dancing Figures on White*, *Musicians*, *Draughts Players*, *Leaping Figure*, *Figure in the Act of Sitting Down*, and *Figure with a Trumpet*. In all, the catalog records 22 painted works and 38 graphic pieces, several times the number of works exhibited by other artists (with the exception of Rodchenko, who exhibited even more than Stepanova). Transporting their works from the studio to the exhibition hall was a complicated operation. They had to pack and deliver several dozen bales of paintings, but this was what they wanted and what stimulated them — to compete with their colleagues not only in the novelty of their works but in sheer quantity too.

Stepanova's compositions, representing the human body in different situations and actions, expressed a variety of spatial planes. Against a pure white canvas these little geometric men bring to mind projects for cybernetic systems. The celebrated collector George Costakis even called them ''robots.'' When placed against a colored ground the figures can be perceived as brief scenes from everyday life, drawn from the imagination. Space and depth are constructed through color and the placement of figures one on top of the other. Here too the facture of the painting is no less bright and rich than in the graphic works. Angled brushstrokes predominate, as in Cubist painting. Still another new kind of cross-wise brushstroke is introduced, but in painting with color this stroke is perceived not as rigid hatching, but as a colored fabric, an ornamental structure.

On October 2, 1920 the 19th State Exhibition opened at the Art Salon located at 11, Bolshaia Dmitrovka Street. Works by Rodchenko and Stepanova were shown in the same room and hung opposite each other. Stepanova wrote in her diary:

The first day there were almost 1500 people. It was extraordinarily lively with masses of people, predominantly the participants. On the second day there were 750 visitors and more artists who for various reasons hadn't made it on the first day. According to the Sub-Division the average number of visitors is about 231. Considering the present state of things, life being what it is, that's almost brilliant. Malevich's exhibition can't even draw 50 people, while some of the previous ones — especially the ''oldies'' — attracted about 20.

At the opening Shor got almost embarrassingly carried away with Anti's and my works. Mine he thought were still unformed, still evolving, lacking definite values, but positive in the sense that they are inviolable, like Anti's. Osmerkin admitted that I'm a real painter, and that he never thought I could paint like that. At the exhibition put on by the Union of New Art he described my graphics and paste-ons as ''charming grotesques.''

In general everyone congratulated me as if it were my name-day, with a benefit performance and so on. Shemshurin thought I overworked my paint — in total contrast to Anti (using paint straight from the tube is the sign of an innovator) — but it makes the subject of the painting boring, something which according to him is in general typical of women's art.

Chagall noticed an enormous difference in the way we both work, in how this reveals our personalities. I have an ungovernable, unbalanced temperament with a good measure of chaos. Anti's is cold, calm, analytic, with a tendency to abstraction. Chagall doubted

Five Figures, 1920 (no. 22). Oil on canvas, 80 × 98.

Interior of the 19th State Exhibition, organized by IZO Narkompros, showing a wall of Stepanova's works, 1920.

Three Figures, 1920. Tempera on paper, 39.5 × 35.

whether Anti could ever have painted the world of objects.

Overall though, it seemed to me that he expressed his admiration fairly sincerely and without any shyness, and, like Shemshurin and Shor, he was really intrigued as to what I'll do next . . . .

Probably nothing else along these lines, I think . . . .

But as the subsequent compositions in this series show, Stepanova did continue along these lines. She began to assimilate figural fragments and faces that were themselves extremely abstracted, to the point of being a geometric schema, a linear skeleton. Another series done in 1921 was based on the idea of emotional and psychological impressions. The figures are transformed into patches that dissolve into the white surface of the page through the use of a dry brush. In their sketchiness and expressive power these drawings recall rock paintings. Construction ceases to be an iron law and gives way to the unexpected emergence of this primitive style. Varvara Stepanova's visual poetry and *Figures* are an odd blending of the investigative, analytical tendencies of Soviet artists in the 20s, with the purely emotional quality of art.

The desire to explain one's work, to demonstrate its aims and problems, is characteristic of many artists who exhibited alongside Stepanova. In their manifestos, slogans and catalog articles, Malevich, Popova, Rodchenko, Stepanova, and Tatlin attempted to specify what was innovative about their discoveries in art. Nevertheless, even for them art remained a field that was far from being fully explored. They succeeded in studying just one part of that territory where, several years later, Soviet design and "production art" were to develop. For this group of artists only one thing was beyond doubt — that art always relied on cognition, experiment and discovery.

Consequently, Varvara Stepanova had every justification for writing in the typewritten catalog to the "Exhibition of Four Artists" (the four INKhUK members Kandinsky, Rodchenko, Sinezubov, and Stepanova) that opened in 1920:

Man cannot live without a miracle. By nature he is fully alive only when he is inventing, discovering, experimenting. The process of discovering a miracle, i.e. the incomprehensible, of unmasking, provides a motive for his spiritual activity, whether it manifests itself as thinking, as working on some construction, or simply as organizing one's private life.

We cry, "Down with aesthetics and taste," though both have already been discredited enough. But, of course, that's not everything, and form alone cannot be and is not the content of art. It is still not discovery.

The formal approach which people are now seeking in art is a tribute to the materialism of our time. Actually, none of us is guided by mathematics when we create art.

Exact knowledge is not enough to make one an inventor, whose imagination and technical skills allow him to realize his work, his invention, the incomprehensible.

Only after he has established a concrete fact does the scientist discover the laws governing his discovery, i.e. only then can he explain it . . . .

Male Figure, 1921. Ink on paper, 43.3 × 30.5.

Female Figures, 1921. Ink on paper, 43.5 × 30.5.

Female Figure, 1920. Linocut.

Men Playing Draughts, 1920 (no. 21). Oil on plywood, 78 × 62.

Figure with a Book, 1920. Linocut.

Female Figure, 1921. Oil on plywood, 74.5 × 44.

Peasant, 1921. Oil on plywood, 100 × 66. Exhibited at the exhibition "5 × 5 = 25".

The social and psychological climate that prevailed in the first years of Soviet power created ideal conditions for the development of innovative concepts of style. In addition to the traditional motifs and applications of Art Nouveau, eclecticism, and the Neo-Russian style, a new trend in style became increasingly apparent in art, architecture, graphics and design. It manifested itself first in Malevich's Suprematism, an artistic concept which had evolved much earlier and had been in existence before the architectural and artistic school of Constructivism. The new trend's second manifestation was the concept of abstract structural and geometric modeling, adopted by the self-styled non-objective artists. Stepanova particularly associated this move — crossing over the boundaries of existing and developing stylistic systems — with the laws that produce different technical developments in different artistic spheres.

The non-objective artists were among the first to insist on adapting many purely scientific and technical categories to artistic creativity, such as the experiment, the structural element, facture, the surface qualities of a painting and, finally, construction. All of these specialist enquiries were to become part of the rapid processes of democratization and social reconstruction. This is why, despite the trying material conditions of the years of War Communism, despite the Blockade, the Intervention and the Civil War, these artists began to visualize the coming socialist society, new cities, residential and public buildings, the objects of the future — and one particular response to these barely formulated social demands was the birth of Constructivism (though it was quite incompatible with the actual state of industry). A quote from the declaration of the Art Production Council (in NKP, 1920) illustrates the social and artistic atmosphere of those years: "The construction of a new socialist life cannot take place without a radical re-organization of the existing outer forms of daily life."

When such unprecedented social and political demands were combined and synthesized with innovative artistic ideas, the phenomenon known as "the art of the 1920s" was born. It is this synthesis which has created a lasting interest in the art of the first Soviet decade, not only among artists and art historians, but among the general public too.

In addition to their experimental investigations into easel painting, those artists who were later to form the first creative organization of designers — the group of Constructivists at IN-KhUK (Gan, Konstantin Medunetsky, Rodchenko, Georgii Stenberg and Stepanova) — embarked on intensive conceptual and theoretical researches, combining art history and the philosophy of artistic creativity.

Stepanova drawing designs for textiles, 1924. Photo Alexander Rodchenko.

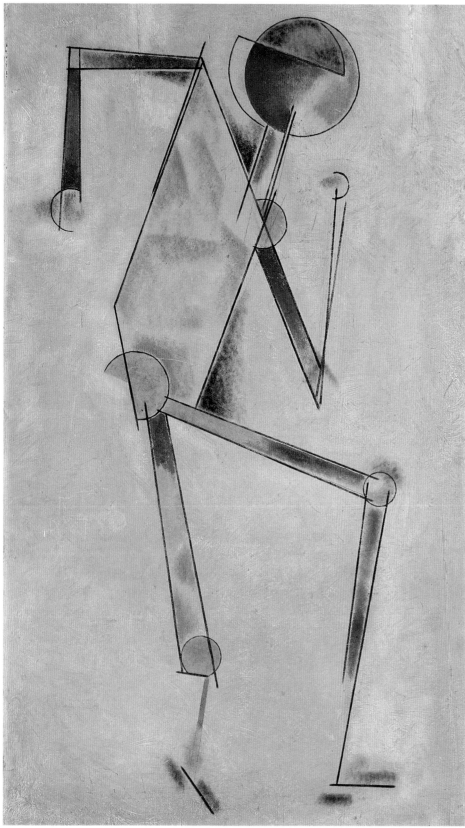

Figure, 1921. Oil on
plywood, 125 × 71.5.

*Two Figures on a Red
Ground*, 1920. Oil on
cardboard,
29.4 × 20.5.

The Institute of Artistic Culture was established in 1920 with Vasilii Kandinsky as its first director. The Institute's goal was to discover the scientific foundations for the interaction and synthesis of the arts, and with this goal in mind, the "elements" of painting, graphic art, sculpture, music and choreography were investigated. Toward the end of the 20s a more materialistic viewpoint prevailed, one which placed greater stress on questions of construction and functional or utilitarian creativity. There evolved a theoretical approach to design, which was subsequently followed by a more practical approach. Rodchenko and Stepanova took an active part in all these efforts. During the summer of 1920 Rodchenko was, in all but name, the head of INKhUK, chairing meetings and selecting the visual material for discussions of particular works of art. And Stepanova, in addition to taking part in all the debates and discussions (among the most important of which was the 1920 discussion on construction and composition), kept almost all the INKhUK minutes. She was an extraordinarily efficient secretary, noting down the whole gamut of opinions expressed by the participants.

INKhUK moved away from investigations into the laws of "pure" art towards a reexamination of the artist's relationship to production. This, in turn, related to the analysis of construction as the central characteristic of form, as the merging of artistic and technical factors. The members of the Group for Objective Analysis at INKhUK turned to the analysis of construction for two reasons. The first was related to the constructive and geometric tendencies in experimental painting of the 20s. The second was the specific factors inherent in a systematic method of analysing works of art. Once having divided the work of art into separate elements, artists were then obliged to investigate the laws governing the organization of these elements within the work. The following laws were discussed: rhythm, composition, and construction; they were then elaborated visually. Thus, the discussion on construction and composition was accompanied by graphic sketches illustrating the issues of "Construction" and "Composition." As an example of "construction," Stepanova presented a schematic head and shoulders image from her *Figures* series, and as an example of "composition," a collage.

Among the definitions of composition which Stepanova proposed was the following: "Composition is a method of organizing elements. The entire compositional process is always constructed upon form, understood as a drawing, a blueprint, or a plan." In the course of the discussion it became clear that "real construction is manifested only in real things operating in real space." The point of departure for analysing a work was the definition of construction posited by the architect Nikolai Ladovsky, as it evolved out of the specifics of engineering and technical constructions: "Technical construction is the combination of material elements shaped according to a defined plan or schema so as to attain an effect of force."

The discussion on construction and composition within the Group for Objective Analysis determined that construction was a means of organizing forms associated primarily with the function of the object and the rational utilization of material. Following from Ladovsky's definition of construction it was concluded that the abstract, unfunctional constructions which artists were continuing to create lacked expediency. In such a situation technical forms attracted the members of INKhUK by the very specific demands of their aesthetics and functionality. The world of industry became a particular standard for constructiveness and expediency. The final conclusions of the Group for Objective Analysis' work already contained an appeal to assimilate utilitarian objects artistically on the basis of the way they were constructed. Artistic, engineering and technical activities should all share a common constructive approach to creativity.

Design for Sports Clothing, 1923.

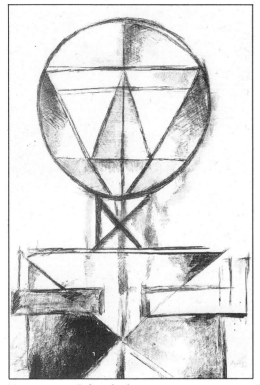

Torso, 1921. Colored ink on paper, 29 × 20.2.

Composition, 1919. Collage.

In the course of 1921-22 several lectures were presented at INKhUK on the subject of construction, Constructivism and "production" art. These were, in order of presentation, Alfred Kemeny's "On the Constructive Works of OBMOKhU" [The Society of Young Artists], Stepanova's "On Constructivism," Anton Lavinsky's "Neo-engineerism," Boris Kushner's "The Role of the Engineer in Production" and "The Artist and Production," and Osip Brik's "What the Artist Should Be Doing Right Now."

Many theoretical questions of design were addressed at lectures and in discussions: the artist's real role in production, the interaction between artist and engineer in planning goods, the specific nature of the "Constructivist's" creative method, the contribution which the designing of abstract spatial constructions makes to the development of "production" art.

Stepanova's paper "On Constructivism" (see the documents section of this book) which she presented an INKhUK on December 22, 1921 is of interest for several reasons: first, as one of the early general theoretical statements about Constructivism; second, as the work of a practical person and an artist who realized that the shift from abstract experiments to practical and utilitarian work was inevitable; and third, as a lecture which raised the problem of artistic continuity and innovation in Constructivism.

The first part of the lecture stressed the fact that Constructivism was not an artistic trend, but was related first and foremost to a method of form-creation. Constructivism was examined as a complex interaction of artistic and inventive activities. These activities must inevitably be artistic in nature since, according to Stepanova, it occurred in those cultural spheres that raised "the question of the external form" of industrial products. But at the same time Constructivism also incorporated qualities of inventiveness, inasmuch as the external form of an object was to be determined by its construction, its original material structure.

In the second and main part of the lecture, Stepanova pointed out how closely the Constructivist artist's creative thinking paralleled the expediency and rationality of developed industrial production. To demonstrate the justice of her thesis on "the overflow of artistic activity into intellectual production" Stepanova pointed first of all to what she considered were the typical characteristics of artists in the past, who created unique works of art in which the ideal of external beauty remained almost unchanged and was mostly concerned with symmetry and the harmony of form. However, Stepanova asserted, scientific and technical developments had produced a change in the ideals of art. As a result, a new principle of development was established, based on the constant renewal of forms. An ideal of beauty "outside time and space" could not be applied to the art of the twentieth century. Moreover, the twentieth-century artist differed from his predecessors in that he was equipped with a knowledge of the objective laws of art and could therefore consciously organize the objective world around him. In this way, Stepanova concluded, by virtue of being a conscious activity, by virtue of its reliance on scientific data and, finally, by virtue of its connection to technology and production, Constructivism became "intellectual production."

Stepanova had already broached the problem of artistic innovation and continuity in Constructivism in 1920-21, in the visual arts programs for the Academy of Social Education (now the N. K. Krupskaia Moscow District Pedagogical Institute). For the Academy art history course Stepanova established a logical chain of development from one artistic trend to the next, treating the history of art as the analysis of different methods of depicting reality. Within such a system "Constructivism" and "production" art were seen as an inevitable and logical stage in artistic development from depiction (the "Impressionist" stage) through an analysis of the norms of form (the "cognitive-material" stage) to the construction of objects. The constructive object, in Stepanova's view, had no need of additional decoration, since the designer had already thought through all its functional details. "In production art the constructive principle should be applied with the utmost precision, so that the need to apply superfluous artistic details to production will disappear."

In Stepanova's programs for the Academy student teachers, theoretical statements on the introduction of art into production and the proximity of the new art to the problems of production were accompanied by practical exercises. The pedagogue should not only be versatile, he should also have mastered some of the more basic skills of design. Therefore, we find in Stepanova's programs such assignments as street decoration for festivals, designing tribunes and arches, decorating banners, walls, and so on. The final assignment was the most complex — making a maquette for a work room or class room, or equipping a school theater or club. Stepanova's students helped stage evening get-togethers for clubs and theaters which Stepanova herself designed. They cut out and sewed sports clothing, the costumes for the Whites and the Reds in the agitproduction *Through Red and White Spectacles* [Cherez krasnie i belie ochki], built sets, and painted slogans. Purely speculative, logical constructs were thus combined with practical experience that dealt with the object itself, its style, construction and image. The Constructivist aesthetic, which Stepanova defined as "a new understanding of beauty, whereby the most beautiful thing is that which is most expedient and constructive," was embodied in her first productions. In her lecture "On Constructivism" and in the Academy program, Stepanova stressed the need for a swift transition from the principle of "art for art's sake," which still dominated much experimental creativity, to elaborating on real design problems oriented toward society.

Constructivism attracted much argument and discussion throughout 1921-22. The most varied and heated opinions were sparked by Gan's positing of three elements in Constructivism: tectonics, construction and facture. Stepanova thought of tectonics as a concept linked on the one hand to ideology and on the other to a specific attitude to construction. Construction was not simply the connecting of elements such as elasticity and weight. It was the creation of a new object, a construct, the birth of a new, expedient organism. From this standpoint, a "construction" was in fact closely linked to the "geological" sources of Gan's category of "tectonics."

In her paper Stepanova explained tectonics, the principal category in this triad, as "undertaking a task for its own sake." The opposed the tectonic to the monumental, which was paralysed and incapable of development. Stepanova's slogan became "the temporary and transient." In production the outer form may easily be changed, therefore the tectonic form is "the principle of endless change." "Within the short-lived significance of each form lies the principle of its further disintegration and evolution."

In the winter of 1921-22 the Constructivists went beyond the phase "from invention to construction," to the next phase, advancing "from construction to production." This development could be seen both in their personal work and in their attempts to introduce production art into the various departments at VKhUTEMAS (as Rodchenko did at the Metal Department, for instance). But this brought new problems. An entry in Stepanova's diary for March 10, 1922 reads: "It's not easy to agitate for Constructivism, but it's even harder to really reject art and begin to work in production."

In the studio of Rodchenko and Stepanova: *(left to right)* the film director Esther Shub, Rodchenko, the graphic artist Alexei Gan, and Stepanova, 1924.

Catalog of the exhibition "5 × 5 = 25", 1921. Cover by Stepanova, 17.5 × 14.

Stepanova typing, 1924. Photo Alexander Rodchenko.

Certainly this first purely theoretical step towards production was very difficult. But even more difficult was finding a concrete area in which these ideas could be applied to technology. For one thing, there were the unprecedented economic problems caused by military intervention and the Civil War, from which the young Republic was only now beginning to recover. "We have triumphed, but we're battle-scarred," wrote Maiakovsky in his poem "GOOD!" [KHOROSHO!]. Furthermore, there was no tradition of artists working in industry. But the desire to apply the principles of Constructivism to real life compelled them to look for any possibility that would allow them to realize their projects — hence the first books and magazines with covers designed by Alexander Vesnin and Rodchenko, Rodchenko's captions to Dziga Vertov's film-chronicle, and the theater sets designed by Popova and Stepanova for Vsevolod Meierkhold's theater.

In the fall of 1921 the exhibition "5 × 5 = 25" took place on the premises of the All-Russian Union of Poets. The participants were the five Constructivist artists Vesnin, Popova, Rodchenko, Stepanova, and Exter, each exhibiting five works, and each announcing their move away from experimental easel painting into design. Each of the five presented the results of his or her experiments. Rodchenko's were the most radical, with three monochrome canvases in blue, red and yellow, plus a line and a grid painting. Stepanova typed about twenty-five copies of the catalog, each of which carried original graphic works by the participants. Stepanova exhibited a continuation of her *Figures* series: *The Peasant*, *Leaping Figure*, and *Standing Figure*. But in contrast with her works of the previous year, here form was rendered not so much by means of a colored surface as by a linear skeleton composed of schematic figures. In the style of her visual poetry, Stepanova hand-colored several posters advertising the first "5 × 5 = 25" exhibition" (paintings only), and the second (graphic works only). This second exhibition included designs for constructions and stage portals by Rodchenko, Stepanova, and Popova, a fact that may well have played a decisive role in Meierkhold's decision to invite Stepanova and Popova to work in his theater.

Ivan Aksenov, poet, translator, and Meierkhold's close colleague, had this to say of the exhibition: "The projects for practical constructions of the future which covered the walls of the Poets' Union seemed to [Meierkhold] quite feasible within the confines of theatrical performance. He saw their purpose as no longer aesthetic but utilitarian, and they would run counter to established aesthetic traditions, making possible his long-time dream of a performance outside the theater, taken out of the box of the auditorium to wherever one pleased: to the square, the foundry of a metallurgical factory, the deck of a battleship."

Poster for the exhibition
"5 × 5 = 25", 1921.
Stepanova's poster for the opening
of the second "5 × 5 = 25"
exhibition (the first consisted of
paintings, the second of graphic
works) was a collage of postcards
and linocut offprints with added
pencil.

Title page for the catalog of the exhibition "5 × 5 = 25", 1921.

Poster for a debate at the writers club on the subject of the second "5 × 5 = 25" exhibition, 1921.

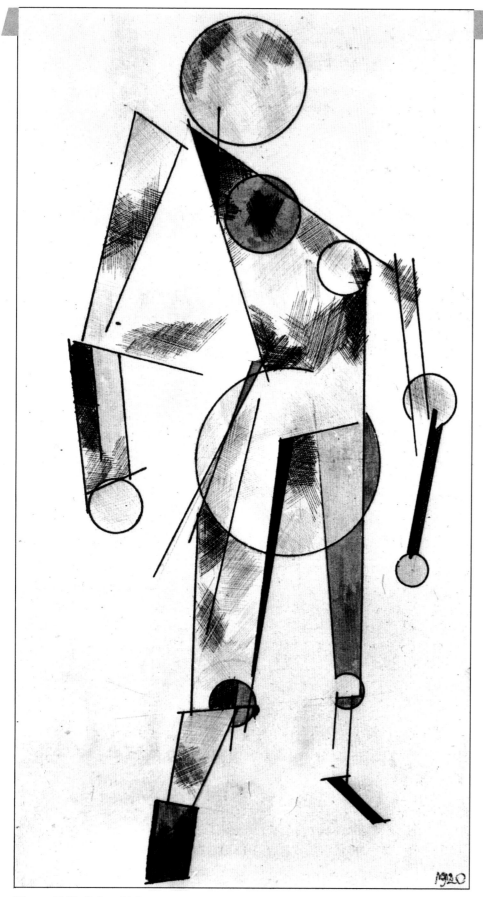

Figure, 1920. Colored ink on paper, 33 × 19.5.

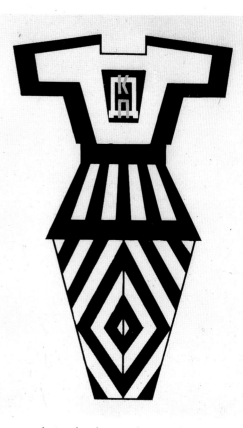

Costume design for theatrical sports demonstrations.
One of Stepanova's early sports costumes, it transforms
the human body into a dynamic geometric composition.

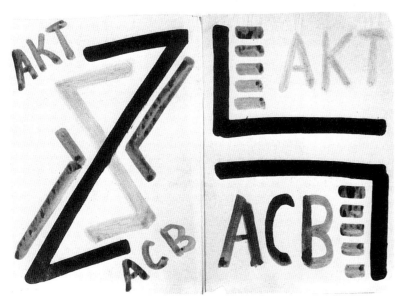

Slogans for the club party at the Academy of Social Education, 1923.

Students of the Academy of Social Education, dressed in sports clothing designed by Stepanova, preparing for a sports demonstration.

Poster for *The Death of Tarelkin*, 1922. Stepanova dedicated her sketch to Vsevolod Meierkhold, the director of the production, which was staged by members of GITIS [State Institute of Theatrical Art].

Scene from *The Death of Tarelkin*, showing the creditors, 1922.

The first production of "theatrical Constructivism" was *The Magnanimous Cuckold* [Velikodushnii rogonosetse] designed by Popova. It took place against the bare brick wall of the theater backdrop, on a light, wooden spatial construction with a wide proscenium in front. For the first time actors were dressed in *prozodezhda*, professional acting clothing that, while comfortable, emphasized the poses and gestures of the characters. Popova helped bring about a fundamental transition: she was no longer decorating the stage, she was mechanizing it.

The production of Alexander Sukhovo-Kobylin's play *The Death of Tarelkin* [Smert Tarelkina] went still further in the active interaction of the actor's performance and the mechanical play of the equipment on stage, for Stepanova made the decorations independent of the stage proscenium, and produced constructive sets and costumes. The historical setting of the play — in the mid nineteenth century — was transformed by its director, Sergei Eisenshtein. Eisenshtein also acted as lab assistant, having already experimented with interpretations of the classics as a popular *balagan* or fairground side-shows, and his production of Alexander Ostrovsky's play *Every Wise Man* at the Proletkult Theater had included tricks by acrobats, jugglers and tight-rope walkers. The psychology of the actors and their basic conflicts were revealed not so much through words as through unusual situations, clowning around, and the

Stepanova demonstrating a folding screen, part of the set for *The Death of Tarelkin*, 1922.

The Death of Tarelkin: costume design for the creditors, 1922.
The characters's chests have on them the acronym GITIS.

Stepanova showing how to operate a collapsible table, designed for *The Death of Tarelkin*, 1922.

Models of the furniture and equipment for *The Death of Tarelkin*, 1922.

rapid sequence of numbers. Such an approach to the production of a historical play necessitated stylistic changes in stage design. The tricks of the *balagan* (sound effects, bulls' bladders, flyswatters, buffoonery) and of circus clownery (acrobatics, quick-change acts, etc.) were woven into the fabric of the action. On a poster for the production, which premiered on November 24, 1922, the words "production artist" were replaced with "constructor." Stepanova proposed a minimum of objects and apparatuses that would provide the players with a maximum of dynamic possibilities. The seat of the chair could be raised and lowered, the stool was supposed to shoot up when someone sat on it, one of the tables fell with a crash on its collapsible legs, while another doubled as a coffin, the meat-grinder which depicted the police station rotated, the screen could be folded and unfolded. The props were painted white to emphasize their open-work construction.

Outwardly the props recall Rodchenko's spatial constructions of 1920-21, constructed on the "principle of identical forms." There are the same standardized wooden slats, the same use of modular prototypes and multiples, the same components joined at a right angle or at forty-five degrees. What Stepanova devised looked like furniture in the most general sense of the word, a skeleton stripped of all ornament and decoration. In other words, the look of the object was defined by its structure.

"The clownery dictated all the functions of the sets and props," Eisenshtein commented. "Instead of sets there was a set of acrobatic . . . apparatuses made to look like furniture." In harmony with the content of this grotesque comedy, ordinary household objects were invested with hidden destructive effects and suddenly began to revolt in the second act, where the main protagonist, Tarelkin, attempts to fake his own death by standing in for someone else, a wealthy and respected man.

In her costume and set designs Stepanova used design graphics to show how the objects were to be prepared technically. The costumes are made of dark blue and gray material, and their geometric cut is already evident in the sketches. The set designs are done on black paper. Strips of white paper, glued one on top of the other in the order in which they will appear in space, simulate the effect of the actual construction made of wooden slats. All the design materials thus demonstrate the close relationship between the graphic methods of design and the technology required to realize a three-dimensional object. The graphic effect of the spectacle on stage is further underscored by the directional lighting, which picks out individual figures and set details in the darkness, while the brick backdrop is lost in the shadows.

According to Stepanova, in a conversation with Gan published in the journal *Zrelishcha*, "In *The Death of Tarelkin* I finally succeeded in showing the utilitarian content of spatial objects. I wanted to produce actual objects — a table, a chair, screens and so on — a total material environment in which the

The Death of Tarelkin: Brandakhlystova's costume.
(Reconstruction by A. V. Epaneshnikova, 1987.)

Scene from *The Death of Tarelkin*, with M. Zharov as Brandakhlystova, 1922.

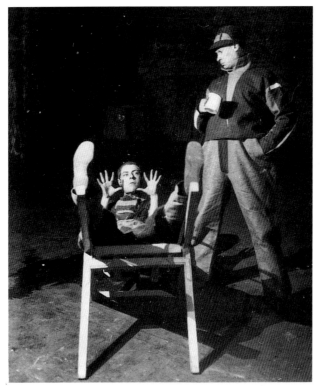

Scene from *The Death of Tarelkin*, 1922, with Varravin and the unmasked Tarelkin, whom objects no longer obey as he topples back in his chair.

The Death of Tarelkin: costume design for Varravin, 1922.

МАСТЕРСКАЯ МЕЙЕРХОЛЬДА — «СМЕРТЬ ТАРЕЛКИНА»

The Death of Tarelkin: P. Galadzhev's caricature of M. Lishin as Varravin, the public servant, holding a flyswatter; published in *Zrelishcha*, 1922.

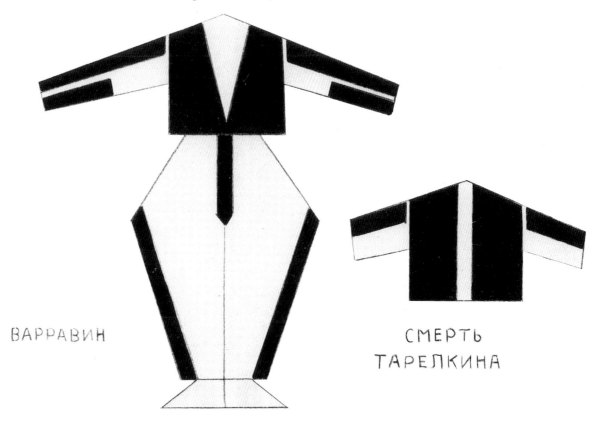

ВАРРАВИН

СМЕРТЬ ТАРЕЛКИНА

The Death of Tarelkin: costume design for Tarelkin, 1922.

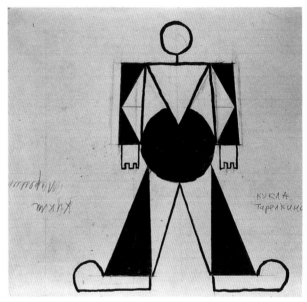

The Death of Tarelkin: designs for various hats, 1922.

The Death of Tarelkin: design for Tarelkin's doll, 1922.
Tarelkin faked his own death with a man-sized doll that
he put into the coffin. The dolls was made of pieces of
colored fabric sewn together and filled with cotton wool.

The Death of Tarelkin: design for Tarelkin's blouse and shirt, 1922.

living human material was to act." Stepanova's costumes helped
the actors to create precise and expressive movements and to
convey the moments of transition from one pose to the next.
When the spotlight fell on the actors their costumes were
transformed into dynamic geometric compositions. In the same
article she defined her goals in costume design as:

"1. To demonstrate and emphasize the inflexions and
movements of the individual parts of the human body.

2. To provide several prototype sports costumes (for the
children, the creditors) and uniforms (for women —
Brandakhlystova, for the military — Okh, Raspliuev and
others)."

This "uniform" principle allowed the director to construct
a rhythmic design for the *mise-en-scène*. All the officials and
creditors were dressed in identical, clearly differentiated
costumes, as if to stress that they belonged to the same sports

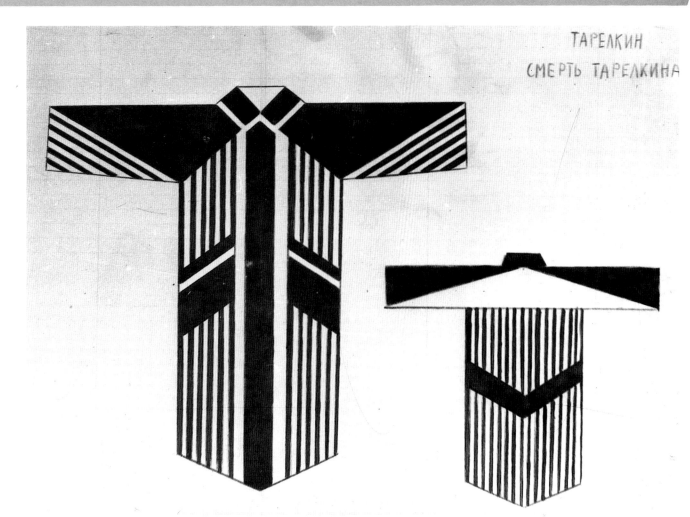

ТАРЕЛКИН
СМЕРТЬ ТАРЕЛКИНА

The Death of Tarelkin: design for Tarelkin's dressing-gown, 1922.

Scene from *The Death of Tarelkin*, 1922. Two creditors appear in Tarelkin's room wearing loose overalls. Tarelkin's doll is lying on the construction that represents the coffin. In the center Tarelkin (played by Tereshkovich), in dressing-gown and cap, tries to pass himself off as his rich neighbor Kopylov.

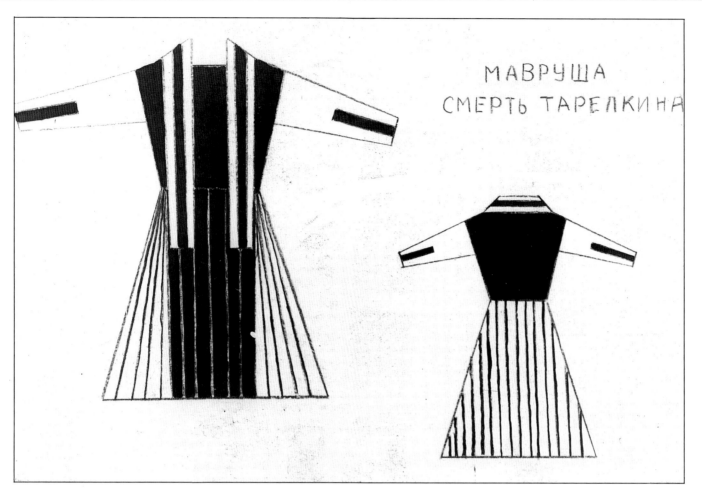

The Death of Tarelkin: costume design for Mavrusha, Tarelkin's cook, 1922.

The Death of Tarelkin: costume design for the two policemen, Kachala-Shatala, 1922.

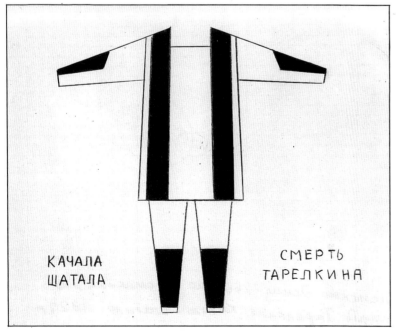

teams. The uniform alluded to the anonymity of bureaucracy and officialdom central to Sukhovo-Kobylin's play.

Several of the characters in the play were clothed not in acrobatic side-show costumes, but in clothing that was completely functional and realistic. The costume worn by Pakhom the porter was a pair of overalls made of scraps of light and dark fabrics, sewn in such a way that the dark pieces were placed in areas most easily soiled and subject to wear. The children modeled sports clothing for young people. All of which transported the play from a historical time into the twentieth century and the fifth anniversary of the Revolution. A classic was unexpectedly transformed into a revolutionary spectacle. All these things made the production of The Death of Tarelkin not only an event in the history of the theater, but in the history of design as well.

Reviews of Meierkhold's production continued to appear for several months. Opinions varied. One author, Arkadii Pozdnev, noted that "the auditorium shook with applause, the newspapers screamed 'it's a flop.' Theater critics drew attention to the virtuoso performances of Orlov as Raspliuev and

The Death of Tarelkin: the meat-grinder; detail in silhouette, 1922.

The Death of Tarelkin: the meat-grinder; working drawings, 1922.

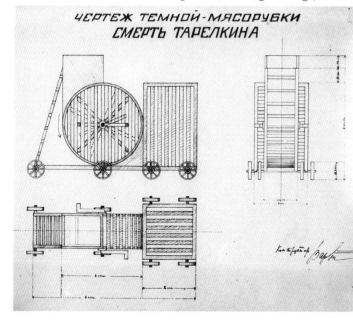

The Death of Tarelkin: the scene at the meat-grinder, which represents the police station where witnesses or those under arrest are kept. The actors clamber up the ladder (*right*), fall into the round barred chamber and end up in the cell (*left*).

The Death of Tarelkin: design for a chair, 1922.

The Death of Tarelkin: design for the swing, 1922.

The Death of Tarelkin: costume design for Brandakhlystova's children, 1922.

The Death of Tarelkin: Brandakhlystova's children on the swing, 1922.

The Death of Tarelkin: the game with the chair, 1922.

ДЕТИ

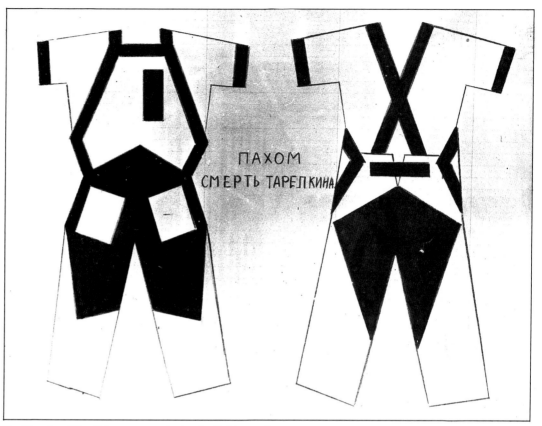

The Death of Tarelkin: costume design for Pakhom, the porter, 1922.

The Death of Tarelkin: sketches
for various hats, 1922.

The Death of Tarelkin: a scene with Pakhom, played by
Losev, 1922. On the transformable table stands an
out-size paper-press.

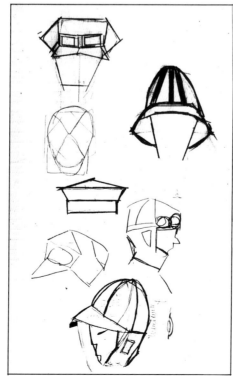

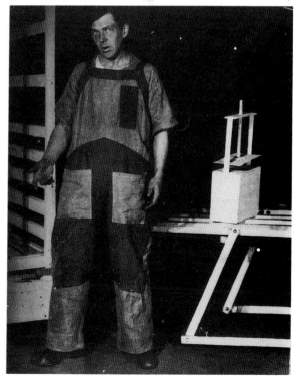

The Death of Tarelkin: designs for the creditors' loose overalls and the transformable table, 1922.

Zharov as Brandakhlystova, and the unsuccessful sets — 'Meierkhold has no luck with artists'.'' The Constructivists, Gan among them, wrote of the Constructivists' victory on stage, of their successful construction of dynamic props and geometric costumes. Practically everyone noted the successful stylistic transition from a nineteenth-century depiction to something new and contemporary in form. Meierkhold himself considered the production seminal, and when, in later years, he demonstrated scenes from his productions he always included scenes from *The Death of Tarelkin*. The director's innovations were made visible thanks to the innovations of the artist.

Stepanova continued to design for the theater. In 1923 she worked on the club performance *Through Red and White Spectacles*, and in 1924 on the agit-performance *An Evening of the Book*, staged at the Academy of Social Education.

In 1926 she was also invited to design the sets for the film *Alienation*, although the screenplay did not allow her to exploit the film as a vehicle for communicating her original ideas about furniture, costumes and props design. For the most part the film's action takes place in living quarters that were typical of the mid-twenties, so that Stepanova had to construct the interiors of communal apartments. Only the scenes that took place

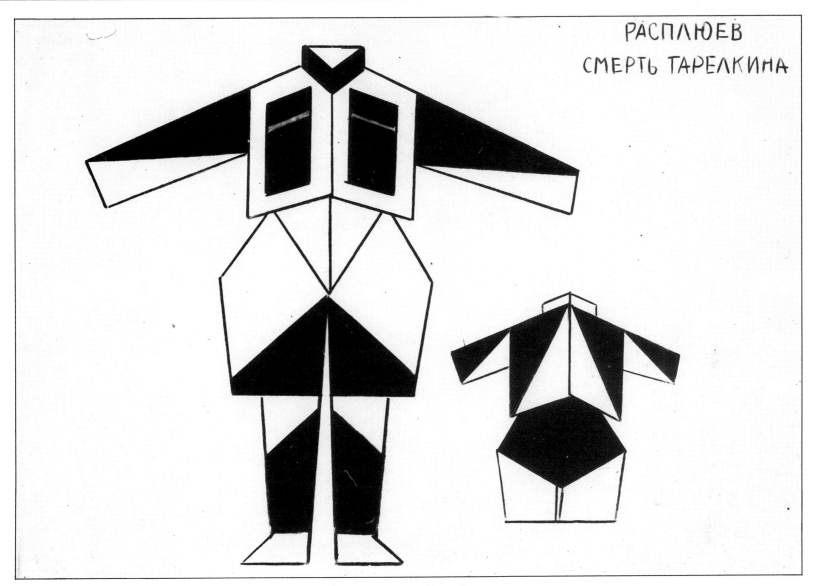

РАСПЛЮЕВ
СМЕРТЬ ТАРЕЛКИНА

The Death of Tarelkin: costume design for Raspliuev, the police supervisor (played by Orlov), 1922.

at the ultra-expensive hairdressing salon, where the negative characters worked, gave her an opportunity to indulge her designer fantasies. Instead of using wallpaper she covered the walls with a kind of structured relief. The stools and chairs were geometric in style, and she also concocted fantastic hairdryers for the beauty salon.

Stepanova's self-caricature as "The Constructor Stepanova,"
1922. The drawing was published in *Zrelishcha*, 1922, with
other material devoted to Constructivism, including two more
caricatures by Stepanova: "The Constructor Rodchenko" and
"The Constructor Alexei Gan." The caricature of Popova,
evidently intended for the same issue, was not published
(*right*).

Double play-bill for *The Death of Tarelkin* and *The Magnanimous Cuckold*,
1922. Both productions were staged by Meierkhold's theater.

Caricature of "The Constructor Popova," 1922. Popova is shown in the
costume of a character from *The Magnanimous Cuckold*, for which
Stepanova designed the set and the actors' "prozodezhda."

The "Exposition internationale des arts décoratifs," Paris, 1925: a detail of the theater section, showing sets and costumes for *The Death of Tarelkin*. Photo Alexander Rodchenko.

Stepanova's textiles at the entrance to the Soviet section of the "Exposition internationale des arts décoratifs," Paris, 1925.

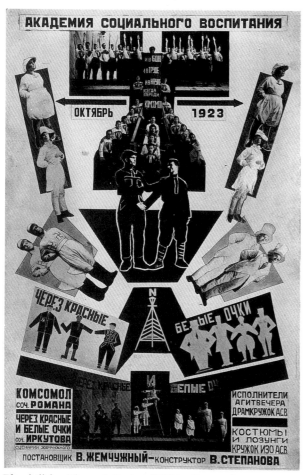

Through Red and White Spectacles: costume designs for the Whites, 1923.

Play-bill for *Through Red and White Spectacles*, staged by the Academy of Social Education, 1923.

Through Red and White Spectacles: costume designs for the Reds, 1923.

Construction design for *Through Red and White Spectacles*, 1923.

Scene from *Through Red and White Spectacles*, 1923.

Sports costume. (Reconstruction by E. Khudiakova, 1986.)

Design for a sports costume, 1923.

Stepanova's most detailed explanation of her credo as a clothes designer is to be found in her pioneering article in *LEF* (1923), "The clothing of the present day — *prozodezhda* [Kostium segodniashnego dnia], illustrated with her designs for sports clothing. The basic principle of designing *sportodezhda* was the application of sharply differentiated, colorgraphic team emblems composed of large forms and contrasting color combinations. Stepanova wrote that in designing *prozodezhda* it was essential to elaborate several basic models which could then be modified to fit a particular profession. *Prozodezhda* thus became the product of mass-production, not an individually handcrafted object. "Individual details are introduced through the material and the detailing of the cut, depending on whether the clothing is for an engineer in a printing shop, on a steamship or in a metallurgical factory."

In addition to *prozodezhda*, Stepanova felt that another type of special protective clothing, or *spetzodezhda* (literally, special clothing) should also be introduced. "A special place within the category of *prozodezhda* belongs to *spetsodezhda*, with its more specific demands and the need for incorporating functional components into the clothing itself. . . . Such costumes could be worn by surgeons, pilots, workers in acid factories, firemen and members of arctic expeditions." In other words, in designing clothes for specific professional groups Stepanova took as her point of departure the wearer's working conditions. She considered that the seams of the pattern, the fastenings and the pockets provided sufficient opportunities for expressing the nature of each profession's clothing. Analysis of the functional demands of clothing enabled her to identify three types: production clothing, special clothing and sports clothing. Within each of these groups she proposed several basic models which, when varied, would provide all necessary modifications. The *LEF* 1923 article on clothing design is of interest not just because it advocates a functional and constructive approach, but also because it contains a number of curious observations on the social nature of fashion: "Fashion, which psychologically reflects our daily life, habits and aesthetic taste, is giving way to clothing organized for working in various branches of labor, for a specific social function, to clothing which can be worn only during the work process, to clothing which has no self-sufficient value outside real life."

Stepanova also felt that the cut of a garment and the design of its fabric should be worked out simultaneously. She devoted an entire article ("From clothing to patterns and fabric" [Ot kostiuma k risunku i tkani], in *Vechernaia Moskva*, 1929) to explaining this idea, and it appeared at a time of keen debate on the direction which the organization of the everyday environment should take, just when the planning of communal housing was beginning under the slogan "For the Socialist reconstruction of daily life."

We are now approaching a point when the gulf separating the fabric itself and the ready-made garment is becoming a serious obstacle to improving the quality of our clothing production. No longer can we

Design for a sports costume, 1923.

Stepanova with her textile designs, 1924. Photo Alexander Rodchenko.

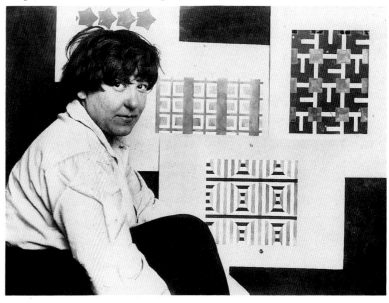

Fabric design, 1924.

Sports costume by Stepanova, modeled by E. Zhemchuzhnaia, 1924.
Photo Alexander Rodchenko.

Design for a sports costume, 1923.

Design for a sports costume, 1923.

speak of putting together a pattern. It is time to move from designing clothing to designing the structure of the fabric. This will allow the textile industry to jettison its present excessive variety, and help it standardize and improve, at long last, the quality of its production.

Stepanova worked for only a year or so at the First Textile Printing Factory, but she managed to design more than 150 different fabrics, of which about two dozen were put into factory production. She was considered one of the foremost experts in organizing textile production. At the end of the 1920s she was invited to design serial models for women's clothing, and in 1929 won third prize at the exhibition "Everyday Soviet Textiles" at the Tretiakov Gallery, Moscow.

For the theoreticians and practitioners of "production" art, and for the students in the production departments at VKhUTEMAS, the fact that Popova and Stepanova worked in a factory as artists designing objects for mass production was the first practical application of the slogan "art into production." Popova's and Stepanova's activity as textile artists was not confined to the design process. Popova worked out models for clothing, while Stepanova taught at the VKhUTEMAS Textile Institute, wrote articles, and agitated for a new attitude among artists toward designing fabrics and clothing.

How did Popova and Stepanova regard their work in industry during these years? In a memo written in 1923 or 1924 for the management of the First Textile Printing Factory, both women tried to outline the artist's sphere of activity in production. The traditional type of artist-draughtsman in the factory had no interest in the technical potential of production, the demands of the market or the application of the fabric they designed. In their memo, therefore, they noted three kinds of artistic activity in production: organizational and supervisory, artistic and constructive, and scientific and research-oriented. They summoned fellow-workers:

1. To participate in the work of the production organs, to work closely with or to direct the artistic side of things, with the right to vote on production plans and models, design acquisition, and recruiting colleagues for artistic work.
2. To participate in the chemistry laboratory as observers of the coloration process . . .
3. To produce designs for block-printed fabrics, at our request or suggestion. [Stepanova is referring to the artist's ability to request changes in the range of goods produced and her right to propose the release of experimental and industrial designs specifically geared to factory production.]
4. To establish contact with the sewing workshops, fashion ateliers and journals.
5. To undertake agitational work for the factory through the press and magazine advertisements. At the same time we may also contribute designs for store windows.

As these five points show, the principles of this proposed plan of action were sufficiently broad to be applied to any concrete area of production. Such a comprehensive attitude was typical of the Constructivists: they used the same terms to

Fabric design, and sketch for a fabric border, 1924.

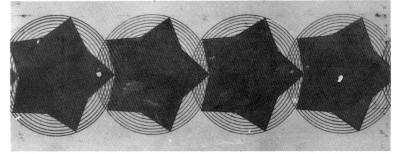

Design for a sign for the First Textile Printing Factory, 1924.

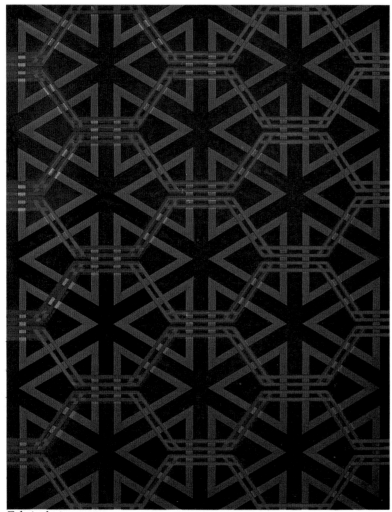

Fabric design, 1924.

Fabric design, 1924.

declare the value of any aspect of artistic work in any field, whether printing, daily life, or education. The memo is also a remarkable expression of the Constructivists' conception of the artist as a coordinator in production, as a specialist interested not only in the design process but also in all the stages of production.

As for the actual process of textile design, Stepanova felt that the artist should design the fabric "from within," starting with the rules governing its weaving so as to attain not just new decorative surfaces, but also fabrics with new physical properties: "the artist's attention should be focused on the processing of the fabric, on developing new types of fabric, and on dyeing it . . . . Just like every other aspect of production, the pattern will be standardized and will eventually be expressed in the processing of the fabric's structure."

However, Stepanova and Popova were unable to implement their ideas at this time. Instead, they had to make do with the technology available to them — simply printing a pattern on the monotone surface of the fabric. Stepanova's fabric designs consist of a multi-level color-field, so that when we look at them we gradually discern forms in the depth of the pattern. Though she uses only one or two colors, Stepanova creates an illusion of several spatial planes existing on the surface. This impression of an almost structural combination of geometric forms arises from the fact that parts of the forms superimposed on each other are outlined but are not colored in. As a rule, Stepanova leaves the points of intersection either white or the ground to show through, thus creating the optical impression of a second plane. The stable, almost crystalline construction on the surface of the fabric brings to mind an urban architectural complex.

The design, as it were, gives visual reinforcement to the fabric. True to her principle, Stepanova treats the design of printed fabrics as a geometric structure applied to the fabric. One of her sketches exactly reproduced on the surface of the print the texture of a fabric woven of thicker threads.

After Popova's death in 1924, Stepanova continued her work with textiles, producing designs more complex in composition. Apart from the purely static aspects of the design, she was attracted by the potential for creating illusions of movement, of forms transmuting into one another (arcs into a circle or triangles into a rhombus). The frequency of the vertical linear rhythms suggests a parallel to the cinematic movement of surface forms, the frequent verticals corresponding to rapid sequences of frames. Unexpected optical effects result, such as those which Victor Vasarely was to explore a decade later in 1934. The secret of these optical formations and vibrations lies in the combination of several intersecting matrices.

Stepanova composed all the geometric forms of her fabric designs with compass and ruler. Only three geometric shapes occur: the circle, the triangle, and the rectangle. On the one hand, these geometric constructions seem to embody ideal forms purified of stylistic elements (though this in itself becomes a stylistic trait). These geometric forms seem universal and fundamental. It might seem that to geometricize a fabric design is an act of violence, and yet as Nikolai Sobolev had demonstrated in his book *The Naboika in Russia* [Naboika v Rossii ; block-printed fabric] (1912), this kind of ornament is rooted in the rich traditions of Russian decorative art. So, unexpectedly, Stepanova's innovative fabric designs proved to be the continuation of a long tradition. The application of geometry to textiles revealed new possibilities for "implanting" such designs into the most unexpected cultural contexts.

A fabric design might sometimes meet with an unexpected reception once it arrived in the store. It happened, for instance, that one of the first designs put into production was similar in its emotional impact to popular Tartar designs. Every single yard was bought up and shipped to Kazan where it was made up into robes. On the other hand, the geometric construction of Stepanova's fabric designs can also be interpreted as the mechanization of the artist's labor, bringing her working methods closer in line with the technology of mass production. Stepanova's geometric fabrics also reflect the world of industry in graphic form. Rather than reproduce mere copies of industrial forms, however, she finds her own plastic means to express the principles of technological form.

The simple geometry of these basic elements enabled Stepanova to reproduce forms even while still working on the sketch, and to build rhythmic structures on the surface. Her work has all the excitement and interest of a pioneer discovering complex combinations made from the simplest forms. Sometimes these combinations resemble natural structures, but even then the compositional law governing each design can be described in precise mathematical terms.

Despite the small number of designs that were actually produced, the influence of Popova's and Stepanova's work on the renovation of textile design both at the First Textile Printing Factory and at other enterprises as well, was significant: "voile and prints have not just become artistically acceptable, they have reached the level of real art, and have brought the rich colors and intense ornament of contemporary art to the cities of our immense Republic," the critic D. Aranovich stated in 1926.

In 1923 Stepanova became professor of composition in the Textile Department of VKhUTEMAS. It was her view (stated in an unpublished document of 1925) that the faculty should turn out "an artist-constructor in the textile industry, not an applied artist; an inventor of style, not an adaptor of foreign and old designs." One method of cultivating a student's powers of observation and ability to influence consumer tastes was the special notebook which Stepanova had every student keep. The students were to go out into the streets and note down the way people dressed and changing trends in fabric designs, then analyse these changes so that they would later be able to formulate design projects of their own.

Another peculiarity of Stepanova's teaching activity in the Textile Department was her efforts to expand the scope of learning assignments, to show the students that their profession was not just confined to the preparation of fabric designs, but also dealt with the design of actual clothing and headgear, such

Fabric design, 1924.

Fabric design, 1924 (variant on color placement).

Fabric design, 1924.

as that worn by postmen. Stepanova even set a special assignment of designing display windows for a fabric store. Her training methods included multiple level constructions, precise articulation of primary geometric elements, and the establishment of links between the ornament and the finished product, the garment.

At the ''Exposition des arts décoratifs'' of 1925 in Paris, Stepanova contributed to several sections: the ''Graphics'' and ''Theater'' sections at the Grand Palais, and the section devoted to decorative art, book design and advertising graphics, and architecture on the Esplanade des Invalides. Rodchenko organized the display of her theatrical work. He set up maquettes from the production of *The Death of Tarelkin* on a special podium and hung costume designs and stills from the production on display panels.

Vivid fabric designs by Stepanova and Popova framed the entrance to the Soviet exhibition area, in an old exhibition hall on the Esplanade des Invalides. With posters by Lavinsky, Popova, Rodchenko, and Stepanova, the exhibition was a celebration of the new Constructivist style, and Stepanova's precise geometric works upheld the overall tone of severity and clarity that characterized the Soviet section of the exhibition.

Fabric design, 1924 (an optical illusion of the surface vibrating and the diamonds moving across the surface of the design).

Fabric design, 1924.

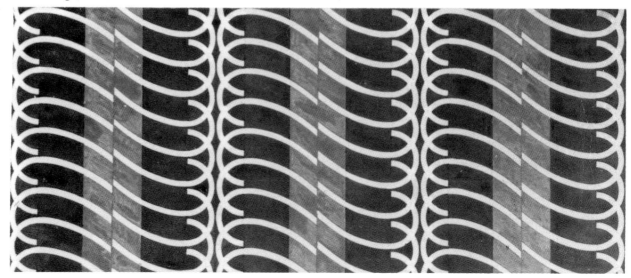

Fabric design, 1924.

Fabric printed with a design by Stepanova, 1924.

Fabric design, 1924. By superimposing semitransparent circles of various colors over each other, an illusion of spatial planes is created, and an impression of dynamism, rotation, and undulating movement.

Stand displaying prize-winning works at the exhibition "Everyday Soviet Textiles," State Tretiakov Gallery, 1927. Two of Stepanova's works were awarded third prize.

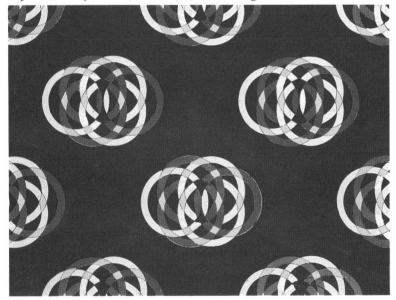

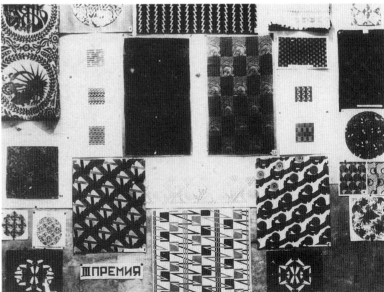

Fabric design, 1924.

Fabric design, 1924.

Stepanova at her desk, wearing fabric designed by Popova. Photo Alexander Rodchenko, 1924.

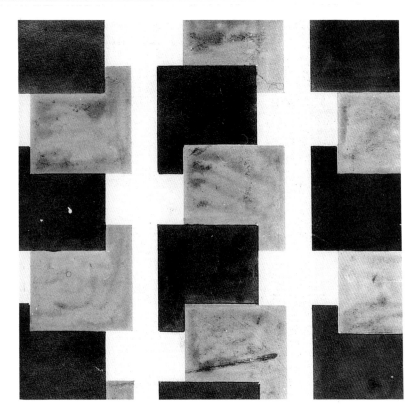

Fabric design, 1924. The design was
produced in two colors, black and gray.

Fabric design, 1924.

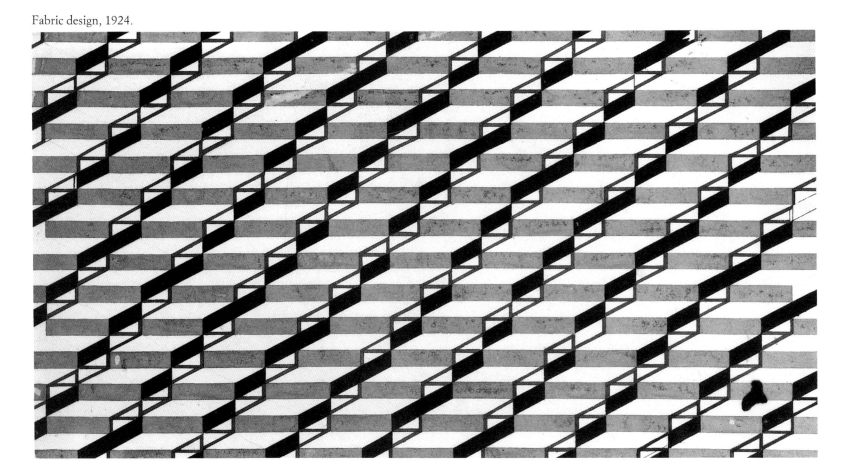

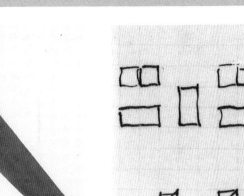

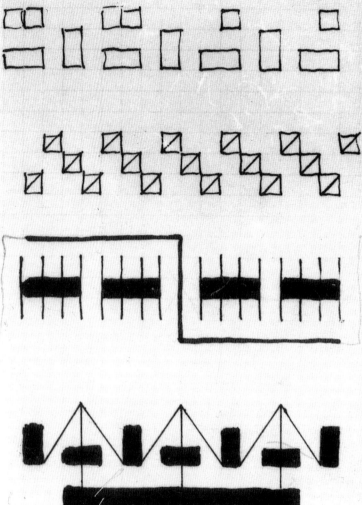

Dress design, 1924. The idea for the design on the fabric, combining plain-colored and decorated areas, evolved out of the dress-pattern itself.

Fabric design, 1924.

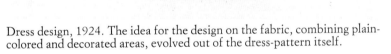

Rough sketches for constructing an ornamental scheme, 1924.

Fabric design, 1924.

Sample of checked flannel produced to a design by Stepanova, 1924.

Self-caricature in a clown costume, 1924.

An Evening of the Book: caricature of Rodchenko in a clown costume of geometrically patterned fabric, 1924.

Fabric design, 1924.

Fabric design, 1924. By moving the halved, concentric circles, Stepanova created a dynamic richness of forms.

Page from the handwritten magazine *Nash Gaz,* from the third
issue on textiles. Popova sets out for the First Textile Printing
Factory with a wheelbarrow full of sketches to have her new fabric
designs approved. Stepanova is carrying some rough sketches to the
factory. The text reads:
"Overheard Conversations"
Anton [Lavinsky]: Where are you off to, Liubochka?
Liubov [Popova]: I'm taking my week's production of prints to the
Tsindel Factory [the old name for the First Printing Factory, after
its former owner].
Anton: How come you're walking lighter today, Varvara?
Varvara [Stepanova]: I'm taking two prints to the Tsindel Factory
so I don't get conceited!

Double portrait of Stepanova and Popova. Photo Alexander Rodchenko, 1924.

Page from *Nash Gaz,* 1924. Caricatures of Popova and Rodchenko.

Fabric design, 1924, conceived as a multi-level constructivist-geometric structure.

Fabric design, 1924, produced in a variety of colors and fabrics such as flannelette.

Fabric design, 1924. This sketch was rejected by the factory management on the grounds that it was "like a metro" (few people in Moscow in those days had the slightest idea of what a metro was).

Display window of the "Fabrics" store, 1924, showing fabrics designed by Stepanova. Photo Alexander Rodchenko.

"Optical" design for fabric, 1924.

Stepanova wearing a dress made of fabric produced to her design, 1924. Photo Alexander Rodchenko.

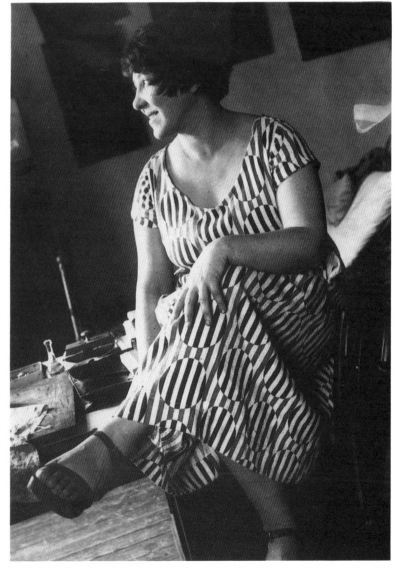

Flannelette sample design, 1924.

Fabric design, 1924.

Fabric design, 1924.

Stepanova in a shawl of fabric produced to her design, 1924. Photo Alexander Rodchenko.

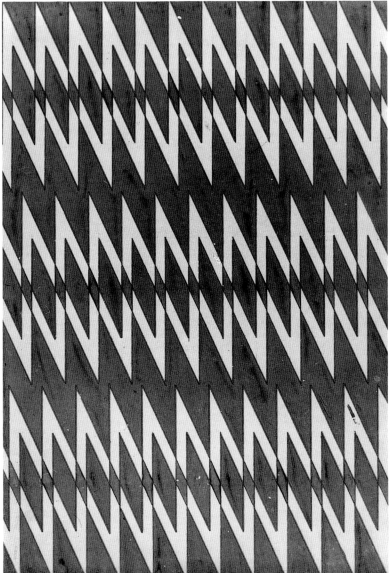

Fabric design, 1924.

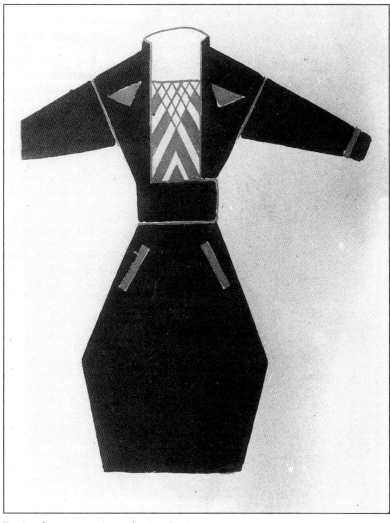

Design for a woman's professional suit, 1924.

E. Khudiakova models her reconstruction of Stepanova's professional suit, 1986.

Designs for women's professional suits, 1924.

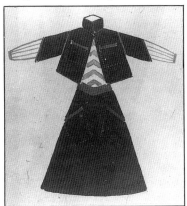

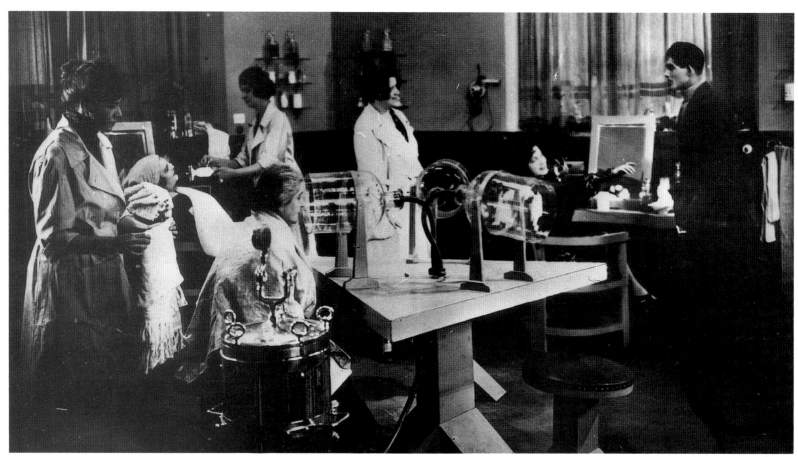

Still from the film *Alienation*, 1926. Sets by Stepanova.

Still from *Alienation*, 1926. The latticed ornament on the wall resembles embossed wallpaper (the only instance of Stepanova's textile designs being used for interior decoration.

Still from *Alienation*, 1926. Defining space using semitransparent fabric for suspended partition-blinds.

Fabric design, 1924.

Stepanova wearing a headscarf of fabric designed by Popova, 1924. Photo Alexander Rodchenko.

Printed fabric sample, 1924.

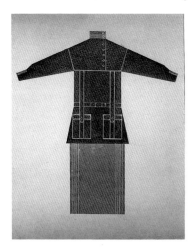

Design for a woman's
"production" suit, 1924.

Woman's "production" suit in black and gray. (Reconstruction by A. V.
Epaneshnikova, 1987.)

Despite the diversity of her interests, the polygraphic arts were Stepanova's most consistent and stable field of activity. She worked on book design for more than thirty years, from 1924 to 1958, and when she joined the Union of Artists of the USSR in 1932 it was as a book designer. She understood the specifics of publishing. The organizational talents essential to both theater design and polygraphy, the ability to compete with specialists in other areas, and to be, as it were, in charge of the situation — all these qualities were characteristic of Stepanova and were most fully revealed in her book design. In the broadest sense of the word polygraphy is also a form of production, for it includes not only the technical aspects of printing, but also calculated intellectual activity. Stepanova was able to maintain both her artistic and her purely human independence even under the very difficult conditions of the 30s, 40s and 50s, when she was obliged to assume the duties of technical editor, publisher, messenger, and editorial secretary. During the 50s, for instance, Stepanova and Rodchenko produced three major photo-albums: *The Cine-art of Our Motherland* [Kino-iskusstvo nashei Rodiny], *Muskovites Fighting for the Motherland* [Moskvichi v boiakh za Rodinu], and *Thirty Years of Soviet Literature* [Sovetskaia literatura za 30 let]. None of them was published, for a variety of reasons: the loss of the originals, change in management, a lack of interest on the part of organizations. Her managerial skills perhaps explain why many remembered her as a kind, considerate person, easy to get along with despite the constant worry over how things would turn out. Those who worked on the preparation of such albums and books felt more at ease when she was around.

Stepanova and Rodchenko began to work as graphic

Stepanova at her desk, 1924. Photo Alexander Rodchenko.

Charlie Chaplin, 1922 (from a series of drawings).

designers in 1923, when they designed book covers, publishers' trademarks and emblems, and advertising posters.

Book design was one of the few concrete areas of "production art" in which Constructivist principles of "the organic entry of art into life" could be realized. Printing was not only one of the most highly developed production areas at that time, but also the most receptive to artistic change — as opposed to the machine construction industry, for example. The graphic approach typical of Soviet design in the 20s found its fullest expression in the book, the poster, and the periodical. At the same time, however, the book is a complex and polyphonic entity, and simultaneously includes two forms of art: literature and graphics. In the early twentieth century Russia's artistic culture developed by close interaction between literature on the one hand, and painting and graphics on the other. Velimir Khlebnikov and Vladimir Maiakovsky come to mind here, the former as an inventor of the word whose poetry affected not only literature, but also painting, graphics and architecture, and the latter as both a poet and an artist, who used the methods of painting to create his poetry, as Viktor Shklovsky noted. At an evening dedicated to Stepanova held in 1974 at the House of Artists, Shklovsky once again stressed this extraordinary duality in the culture of the 20s and 30s. The art of those years, he said, sprang from the "reinterpretation of both painterly and literary principles."

Rodchenko and Stepanova had many literary acquaintances. Rodchenko remembered Khlebnikov from when both of them worked on the decoration of the poets' Café Pittoresque in 1917. (Rodchenko designed the unusual light fixtures, while Khlebnikov had been commissioned to write a sketch for the Café's opening night.) Rodchenko and Maiakovsky met in 1921 at an OBMOKhU exhibition, where Rodchenko showed a series of astonishing spatial compositions resembling soaring space-ships. But long before they became acquainted with Khlebnikov and Maiakovsky, Rodchenko and Stepanova had been following all the new trends in the literary world and knew the latest anthologies of Futurist poetry.

In March 1923 the first issue of the journal *LEF* appeared. It was oriented equally toward writers and artists: the artistic "object" and the literary "object" were on an equal footing. Contributors to the journal included not only the writers and poets Nikolai Aseev, Kushner, Maiakovsky, Petr Neznamov, and Sergei Tretiakov, and the critics and theorists of production art Boris Arvatov, Osip Brik and Nikolai Chuzhak, but also the artists Rodchenko and Stepanova. All issues of *LEF* (*New LEF* [Novyi LEF] after 1927) — more than twenty covers — were designed by Rodchenko. In addition to the "Program," "Theory," and "Practise" sections, the journal also published literary, artistic and design material. Under the heading "Works of a Constructivist" readers could see Rodchenko's new covers for books by Gan and Aseev, and Stepanova's sports clothing and fabrics. Stepanova wrote on an exhibition of design projects carried out by Rodchenko's students as part of their course work.

From the point of view of Constructivist book design, Stepanova's series of engravings depicting Charlie Chaplin deserve particular attention. In 1922 the third issue of the journal *Kino-fot* appeared, edited and published by Gan, a friend of Rodchenko and Stepanova, and one of the members of the First Working Group of Constructivists at INKhUK. The issue was devoted almost entirely to Charlie Chaplin, and included articles by the famous film director Lev Kuleshov and the theather director and playwright Nikolai Forreger, and a manifesto by Rodchenko, all exhorting directors, artists and actors to study Chaplin from the perspective of his constructive movements, his clowning, and his acting. "Chaplin is always precise. He ignores decorative gestures for their own sake. It is always clear where his work is going and why," wrote Forreger in this *Kino-fot* issue.

All these statements were illustrated by Stepanova. Why were actual drawings used rather than stills from Chaplin's movies? Because graphic means allowed the artist to condense and concentrate Chaplin's plastic language, the rhythmic pattern of his gestures, his gait, his poses. Here Stepanova's experiments on the *Figures* series of 1920-21 stood her in good stead. The geometricization of the human body, plus a few typically Chaplinesque attributes (geometric bowler hat, cane, letters) conveyed the general ideas and principles expressed in the articles on Chaplin. It also clarified the connection between the experiments of this American actor and director and the innovations in the Soviet visual arts of the early 20s. But it was not just the theater and the cinema that included Chaplin in their arsenal, for artists too adopted him as the hero of a new life built upon expedient and constructive principles.

In 1923 Rodchenko and Stepanova embarked on a number of book design projects. There was such an abundance of commissions that in order to keep up with them all and coordinate their production, the theme, character, and realization of each commission had to be recorded clearly and simultaneously. Stepanova also dealt with all the paper work. For the most part all these commissions were Rodchenko's concern, although many designs were carried out collaboratively and a number of covers came out with the initials S. V. — Stepanova Varvara. Over a three-year period 322 commissions were accepted, of which about a quarter were by Stepanova. In these years Rodchenko and Stepanova were involved in designing

Charlie Chaplin, 1922. Design for an engraving.

Cover for Charlie Chaplin, 1926. Unpublished.

Charlie Chaplin Turning Summersaults, 1922.

Charlie Chaplin Turning Summersaults, 1922.

Alternative cover design, 1922.

Cover for the magazine *Kino-fot*, no. 3, 1922.

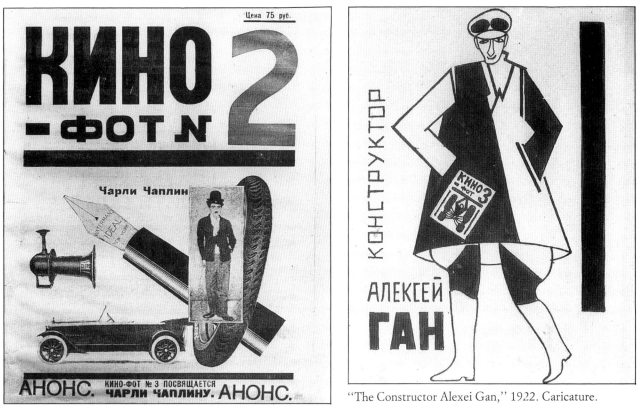

Cover for *Kino-fot*, no. 2, 1922.

"The Constructor Alexei Gan," 1922. Caricature.

Rodchenko and Stepanova, 1923.

ШАРЛО КЛАНЯЕТСЯ.

Sharlo Takes a Bow, 1922. Woodcut.

books and periodicals, decorating display windows and book kiosks, packaging, and advertisements. Of these commissions 117 were directly related to book design. Fifty covers were commissioned by the "Transpechat" [Transportation] publishing house, and thirty by "Gosizdat" [The State Publishing House]. The remaining commissions came from other publishing houses such as "Molodaia gvardiia" [The Young Guard], "Krasnaia nov" [Red Virgin Land], and "Krug" [The Circle]. Comparative statistics show that Rodchenko and Stepanova worked primarily on two types of book: scientific and technical books for the "Transpechat" publishing house, and literature — the poetry anthologies and first editions of works by Maiakovsky, Aseev, and Osip Mandelshtam. The remainder of their work consisted of commissions from publishing houses and trade organizations for advertisements and marketing items such as kiosks, display windows, cases for transporting and selling books, signboards, emblems, posters, and even special headgear for book vendors.

Among the company trademarks which Stepanova designed were those for the "Zemlia i fabrika" [Land and Factory] and "Molodaia gvardiia" publishing houses. Each was based on a relationship between letters and geometric elements, a total composition also evident in her design for magazine titles. The text for the "Gosizdat" advertising posters was written by Maiakovsky. In one case Stepanova based her composition on a diagram showing the rise in the number of books published, in another she used the enlarged image of a book with symmetrical print, while in a third she combined a photograph with a flat graphic form. Thanks to the documentary photo-portrait, the poster becomes more concrete, its exhortation — "He who can read and write will improve the peasant economy, use Gosizdat textbooks to teach your children" — more compelling.

In preparing the initial sketches for book covers and posters that incorporated photo-montage, Stepanova often posed for Rodchenko's camera in the guise of a Komsomol girl in a head-scarf, or as a book-pedlar with a pile of publications under her arm.

Advertising graphics during the 20s was not simply another area of activity for these versatile artists. The advertising poster in these years used both the narrative and illustrative forms of the book, while simultaneously enriching the graphic scheme with bold print, and, as it were, bringing the book closer to the viewer.

Maiakovsky, Rodchenko and Stepanova did much to propagate general knowledge, universal literacy, and the book through their poetry, posters, and graphics. There was a mass campaign to make the population literate (in 1926 the literacy statistics were already 56.6%, double what they had been in 1897). Book fairs and sales of books on specific subjects were held regularly, and there were even theatrical performances and evenings devoted to the book.

Stepanova actually contributed to one of these, *An Evening of the Book* [Vecher knigi] in 1924, and she also designed the supplementary brochure entitled *An Evening of the Book in*

Man on a Propellor, 1922. Woodcut.

Chaplin Next to an Airplane, 1922. Woodcut. The illustrations for *Kino-fot* were printed from woodcuts executed by professional engravers, but for the engravings from the *Chaplin* series Stepanova was directly involved in transfering the design onto the block.

Design for a signboard for the Gosizdat bookstore (in collaboration with Rodchenko), 1924.

Advertising poster: "Adresses of Libraries," 1924.

Design for a signboard for the "Molodaia gvardiia" publishing house, 1924.

"Molodaia gvardiia," 1924. Design for an advertising flyer.

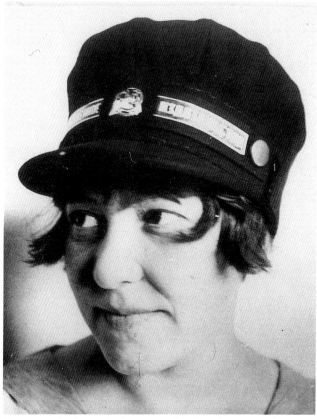

Stepanova in the peaked cap worn by the salesmen at the Gosizdat bookstore, 1924. Photo Alexander Rodchenko.

Stepanova in the beret worn by the saleswomen at the Gosizdat bookstore, 1924. Photo Alexander Rodchenko.

Trademark for the "Zemlia i fabrika" publishing house, 1924.

Opening scene from *An Evening of the Book*, 1924 (text: B. Irkutov and Nikulin; production: Zhemchuzhnyi).

An Evening of the Book, 1924: the intermission.

the Clubs of Youth (*An Experiment in the Mass Artistic Agitation for the Book*). This contained a sample scenario written by Vitalii Zhemchuzhnyi and photographs of scenes from the performance: "The material printed here for the *Evening of the Book* was elaborated on the initiative and directives of the Komsomol group at the Krupskaia Academy for Communist Education. The first performance utilized the resources of the drama, choral and art circles within the Academy's club, and was repeated several times for Red Army and workers' organizations."

An Evening of the Book (directed by Zhemchuzhnyi and designed by Stepanova) presented a conflict between the heroes of old pre-Revolutionary and new revolutionary books. Interspersed with comments by clowns, the characters stepped one by one out of the pages of a gigantic book. The evening ended with the victory of the revolutionary heroes and a parade of libraries and new editions. *An Evening of the Book* was a unique attempt to combine the theater with graphic design, to present the book as a tangible material object, to show the reality and effectiveness of literary characters, and to create a spatial image of the book.

Stepanova made her debut as a book designer in 1924, designing "low-prestige" books for the "Transpechat" publishing house. But even in these brochures on the rationalization of railroad services, rolling stock and so on, the artist showed her individuality in the masterly graphic combination of long and complex titles, and the accentuation of their meaning through the size and shape of the print.

In Constructivist book covers the printed title and author's name often takes up the entire page. The letters are set close together, are piled on top of each other, and exist not so much on the surface of the page, as one behind the other. In the same way, the style of Constructivist printing evolved out of a very specific attitude. Its trademark was the sanserif grotesque, the treatment of which frequently varied from cover to cover, since the print was not composed of ready-made elements such as we have today in Letraset, but each time was drafted anew to fit the required format. In sharp contrast to the classical print-styles with serifs, the sinuous letters of Art Nouveau, or the Neo-Russian variations on old Slavic script, the grotesque had a bold, "democratic" and, most important, a constructive look to it. When they blocked out these letters the artists emphasized their rectangular skeleton and modular basis. The resulting script, combined with the precise and geometric arrows, exclamation marks and other attention-drawing elements, created that specific montage, that technological style identifiable with the polygraphic work of Gan, Rodchenko, Gustav Klutsis, Popova and Stepanova.

Almost all Stepanova's covers from the mid-1920s are signed either with her surname or with the initials S. V. The Constructivists attached great significance to the authorship not only of their own projects but also of mass-produced works. The artist's surname was to function as an advertisement for this new field of design, and to emphasize that the Constructivist artist worked on all kinds of projects related to the produc-

An Evening of the Book, 1924: the clowns.

Poster for *An Evening of the Book*, 1924.

An Evening of the Book, 1924: the red imps (the heroes of a tale by Blokhin) and Kerensky.

An Evening of the Book, 1924: the red imps disarm Pinkerton and Sabaoth.

Cover for *An Evening of the Book* ("Krasnaia nov," 1924).

Stepanova "with books," 1924. Photo for a cover sketch of *An Evening of the Book*. Photo Alexander Rodchenko.

Scene from *An Evening of the Book*, 1924.

An Evening of the Book, 1924: the hero of each book stands in front of its cover.

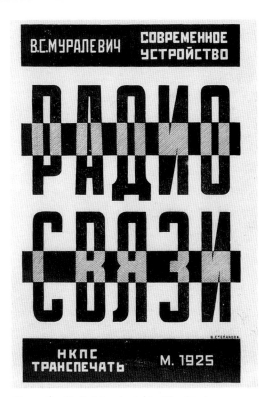

Cover for V. S. Muralevich's *The Modern Wireless Apparatus* [Sovremennoe ustroistvo radiosviazi] ("Transpechat," 1925).

Cover for E. P. Zalessky's *Mountain Paths* [Gornye dorogi] ("Transpechat," 1925).

tion of objects.

"Technology and industry have confronted art with the problem of construction as an active funtion, rather than as a contemplative graphic quality," Stepanova wrote in 1921, in the catalog to the "5 × 5 = 25" exhibition. This technical and technological enthusiasm for graphic modeling had an inevitable effect on the way artists related to their work tools. In Stepanova's later work the handwritten script and the graphics are replaced by mounted, ready-made components, while in the second half of the 20s she made increasing use of photography. In one instance the photographs serve as a documentary account of events, in another as a precise instrument for the plastic modeling of time and space.

In 1926 Rodchenko and Stepanova experimented with photographs to illustrate Tretiakov's book of children's poems *Autoanimals* [Samozveri]. Stepanova used standardized cardboard components to make little folding figures that could be taken out of the book and used as a children's game. Each child could then play out their own variations on their own scenario. The dolls were positioned on a table, spotlit and photographed. Tretiakov's poems dealt with a boy's fantasy about being transformed into an ostrich, a horse, or some other beast, hence the book's title. The standardized dolls provide a visual sequence that parallels the story. In the photographs we see how the arrangement of the figures against a black ground creates an effect of the real space described in the verses. The "auto-animals" are made of both flat planes and cylindrical volumes. When photographed the planes are perceived as being in sharp contrast, the cylinders as soft with transitional half-tones. The camera concentrates on the most volumetric and clear part of each figure. For the first time in Stepanova's and Rodchenko's work photography becomes an arena for the synthesis of the arts: literature, design and photography.

The book was not published, but the text was printed in the journal *Pioneer* and the photo-illustrations by Rodchenko and Stepanova were included in the journal *New LEF*, no. 1, 1927. The Rodchenko-Stepanova archive includes a letter from Chuzhak, a LEF employee, to the "Molodaia gvardiia" publishing house with the following proposal: "Please come to an agreement with the artists A. Rodchenko and V. Stepanova over the preparation of drawings to the text of S. Tretiakov's children's book *Autoanimals*. In view of the artists' high qualifications as well as their adoption of photographic methods in addition to painting, I ask you to be flexible in your negotiations with them."

Stepanova's first experience in collaborating with editor, authors, and printing-house came in 1926-27 during her design work for the journal *Soviet Cinema* [Sovetskoe kino]. Rodchenko was also doing his first photographic experiments at this time (his foreshortened shots using double exposures and scenes from the *Autoanimals* series were published in the same journal under the heading "Photos in Film"), and his and Stepanova's first test pieces as film designers were illustrated in the journal as well. Rodchenko, Stepanova and their colleagues thus discovered one more vehicle whereby they could propa-

Rodchenko's and Stepanova's studio, 1924: (*left to right*) Rodchenko, Zhemchuzhnaia (wife of Zhemchuzhnyi), O. Rodchenko (Rodchenko's mother), Shub, Stepanova.

Cover for L. N. Bernatsky's *Conditions for the Stability of the Earth's Masses* [Usloviia ustoichivosti zemlianykh mass] ("Transpechat," 1925).

Unpublished cover for A. Menshoi's *You and Me in Berlin* [My s vami v Berline], 1924.

China [Kitai], 1924. Heading.

Afghanistan, 1924. Heading.

Cover for "Transpechat's" catalog, 1925.

Cover for N.O. Roginskii's *S.Ts.B.*
("Transpechat," 1925).

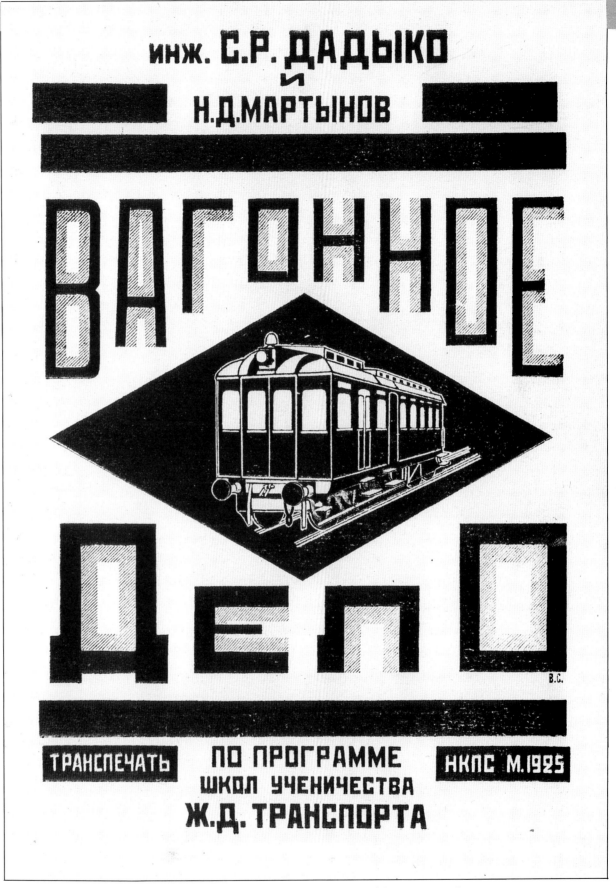

Cover for S. R. Dadiko's and N. D. Martinov's *Rolling Stock* [Vagonnoe delo] (''Transpechat,'' 1925).

Stepanova posing for a poster, 1924. Photo Alexander Rodchenko.

gate the ideas of Constructivism and publicize their new experimental projects.

Characteristic of Stepanova's early polygraphic design is her interest in the imposition of the page surface, in graphically accenting a text where the meaning is of greatest importance — something very apparent in *Soviet Cinema*, where she used up to five different print styles. This allowed her to immerse the reader in the world of information. Editorials, reviews, theoretical statements by film-makers — all this information was emphasized with various accents such as solids, frames, and so on. Stepanova paid close attention to every part of the journal, whether text or photographs. She would often mount small horizontal photos on the pages as a visual reminder of the flickering images on the screen. The geometric structure of the lines and the rectangular shape of the photographs complemented each other on the covers and the spreads. The saturated black solids helped to brighten the grey impression produced by the crude block. The number of lines in the polygraphic screen was no longer of prime importance for the perception of the composition as a whole, since the field of vision was constantly filled with the contrasting solid, which was many times larger than the dots of the screen.

The arrival in Moscow of the director of New York's Museum of Modern Art, Alfred Barr, coincided with the screening of many films by Eisenshtein, Kuleshov and Vertov, and the publication of Rodchenko's experimental photos in *Soviet Cinema*. This led Barr to write in his diary that the Russian avant-garde had moved entirely into film-making, which he interpreted as a move toward a more active and influential art form. He considered Lenin's words that "of all the arts, for us the most important is the cinema" prophetic, in that the most talented directors, artists and playwrights were now converging on the cinema. His inspection of Rodchenko's and Stepanova's work in their studio convinced him that they were approaching photography as a technically precise and reliable illustrative instrument. Later, in his article "LEF and Soviet Art" he noted Stepanova's innovations as a specialist in the montage and imposition of illustrated publications.

From the second half of the 20s Stepanova began to pay increasing attention to the type-setting of graphics. She and Rodchenko now clearly expressed their respective areas of expertise within their mini-collective: Rodchenko honed his skills as a master of sharp graphic compositions and as the "inventor" of a style, who unexpectedly transformed expressive spatial structures into useful and functional objects. Stepanova emerged more and more as a technician, spending much of her time in the editorial office or the print shop. On many occasions she actually produced the sketches for covers, drafting the letters and forms from Rodchenko's hurried sketches on graph paper. From the start, graph paper served as a module for the composition's articulations and rhythms, providing a precise graphic schema.

Stepanova worked on the journals as artist, mock-up designer and art editor, and often as a technical editor too. She produced maquettes for the journals *Soviet Cinema, Book and*

Advertising poster: "He who can read and write improves peasant economy; teach your children with Gosizdat's textbooks," 1925. Text by Maiakovsky.

Rodchenko and Stepanova. Photo-illustrations to Sergei Tretiakov's book for children, *Autoanimals*, 1926.

Rodchenko and Stepanova. Photo-illustrations to Sergei Tretiakov's book for children, *Autoanimals*, 1926.

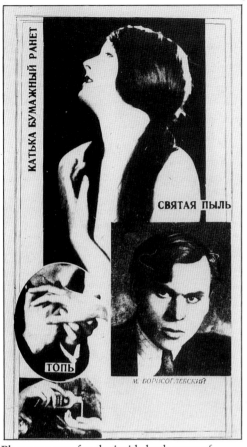

Photomontage for the inside back cover of
Book and Revolution [Kniga i revoliutsiia],
1929: "Katka the paper rennet." A parody of
"railroad reading matter" novels.

Cover for *Book and Revolution*, nos. 15-16, 1929.

Revolution [Kniga i revoliutsiia], *Class Struggle* [Borba klassov], *Radio Listener* [Radioslushatel], *Red Student Life* [Krasnoe studenchestvo], *Literature and Art* [Literatura i iskusstvo], and *Shift* [Smena].

A special design style was worked out for the journal *Book and Revolution*. The writer and journalist Vasilii Katanian used to say that there were only three people in the Soviet Union capable of producing such a journal: Rodchenko, Stepanova, and Gan. Stepanova produced the maquette, using ready-made type-setting elements for the type-face, the solids, and the rules. Frequently she would also select the photos, either placing them in the margins or incorporating them in the text. As a total work of polygraphic art, the life of the journal began in the printing-house with the preparatory lay-out and montage components.

Book and Revolution had a small format, but it contained a good deal of text, facts, and diverse information. Only Stepanova's skill and familiarity with the job of literary and artistic editors, therefore, enabled her to arrange all this information — and to produce the most unexpected comparisons and combinations. Some articles could be read alongside reviews of the same articles and bibliographies on the same topic. Stepanova used type-face, imposition, and jobbing elements to enliven the text. For in addition to simply varying the construction of the type page (in one, two or three columns), and using up to four distinct and different sized type-faces, she also made sure that all the rules of this "game" were strictly adhered to. Excerpts from articles and letters were always in italics, the word "bibliography" was always set vertically in the margins, the editorial was in a single wide column, and the polemics section was in three columns with complex jobbing printing.

In 1929, on the initiative of Katanian (then secretary-in-chief of the journal *Red Student Life*, Stepanova experimented with a new composition for the newspaper *Komsomol Truth* [Komsomolskaia pravda]. Katanian later recalled how Stepanova "was given an issue of *Komsomol Truth*, or rather the type-setting of it. Instead of dividing it up or parcelling it out, they gave it to Varvara. Varvara arrived at night, sat there until morning, and re-imposed everything her own way. After she had re-imposed the issue and made her own headings, it turned out that 25-30% more material could be accommodated in the paper." Katanian explained how she had come up with this additional space: "How did she do her headings? Let's take 'Events in Algiers:' even within this heading the most important words were singled out, for instance, the word Algiers. I remember *Komsomol Truth* didn't follow up on this, didn't want to risk it. Even so some of her headings were adopted, and if you look at an issue of the journal from the early 1930s, you will see that the date — say March 27 — is written with a big '27', a smaller 'March' and an even smaller 'year', since the most important factor is the day."

A second instance of Stepanova's purely design-oriented approach to polygraphy was the magazine *Red Student Life*. "Usually a newspaper is folded in half," wrote Katanian. "We decided instead to fold it so that one page would contain two-

Photomontage for the inside back cover of *Book and Revolution*, 1929: "The Cucumber King." A parody of "railroad reading matter" novels.

Sketch of a cover for *The Soviet Screen* [Sovetskii ekran], 1929.

Cover for *Red Students*, no. 10, 1929.

thirds and another would be folded to half of this page. It was a great idea — and the editor-in-chief approved — since articles could be printed on the large pages and the chronicle section on the small ones. Very large photos could be included in one area, and tiny announcements that could be read on the bus in another.'' But because of complications in approving a standard for the new format, only one issue was published in this way, and in her later work Stepanova went back to the old format.

Stepanova was acutely aware of the changes in design style taking place in the late 20s. The large, rough-hewn geometric forms of Constructivist graphics began to be replaced by a more slender graphic treatment. In 1931 Stepanova designed the collected works of Nikolai Aseev — small red volumes done in the style of *Book and Revolution*. There were much the same accenting devices, rules, and printing graphics that marked the ''Transpechat'' books of the early 20s. Perhaps the difference lay solely in the slender lines and type, and the predominance of the white margin on the page and cover. We recall that in Rodchenko's and Stepanova's early polygraphic works the reverse was the case, with the paper loaded with a maximum of color and tone. The white margin only occasionally peeped through the gaps between letters, solids, and arrows. Perhaps, too, this new effect arose from the roundness of the print. But whatever the reason, Aseev's ten volumes mark a stylistic turning-point in book graphics. To some extent this foreshadows the design style of the 1930s, with its streamlined, rational treatment of the smallest details. The typeface Stepanova proposed was based not on the capital letters used in severe Constructivist graphics, but on lower case letters, flexible and rounded. In the upper portion of the plain red cover the author's surname ''Aseev'' is printed in silver, the A magnified, shining, and streamlined like a perfect airplane component.

An era in graphic design was over. Other pages in the history of the Soviet book were about to open. In their collaborative work on photo-albums, Rodchenko and Stepanova now began a new phase in their art, characterized by the use of photomontage and photography in book design. Stepanova expressed her own attitude to this in an unpublished article of 1929 called ''Photomontage'' [Fotomontazh]: ''The leftist artists who have moved from easel painting into industrial production have been obliged to make fundamental changes in their approach to mechanization, and to the question of documentary precision. This has forced them to resort to the camera as the only means of conveying reality.''

In 1932, the last year of the First Five-Year Plan, the publishing house Ogiz-Izogiz (which specialized in printing illustrated material) put out the album-folder *From Merchant Moscow to Socialist Moscow* [Ot Moskvy kupecheskoi k

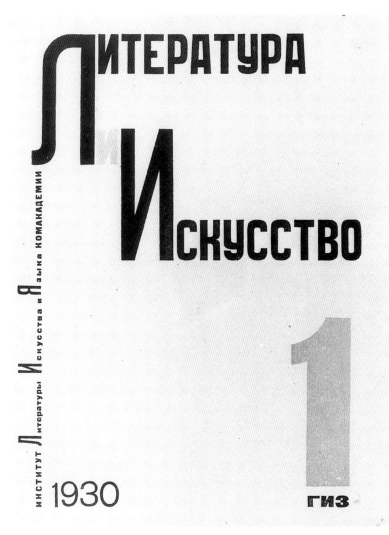

Cover for *Literature and Art* [Literatura i iskusstvo], no. 1, 1930.

Cover for *Modern Architecture* [Sovremennaia arkhitektura], no. 4, 1929.

Stepanova's identity cards issued by Dom Pechati (now the Union of Journalists of the USSR) and Partizdat, 1932.

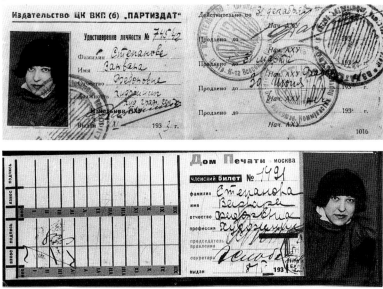

СОВЕТСКОЕ 2

КИНО

Cover for *Soviet Cinema*, no. 2, 1927.

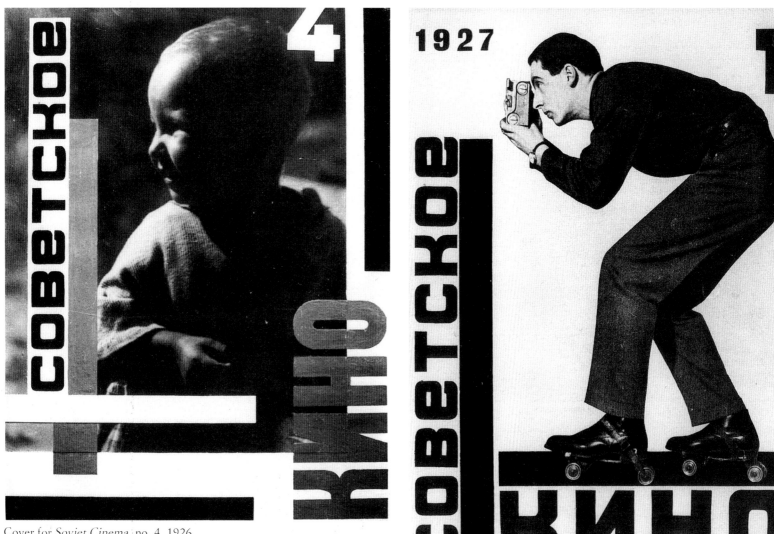

Cover for *Soviet Cinema*, no. 4, 1926.

Cover for *Soviet Cinema*, no. 1, 1927. The cover shows Kaufman on roller skates carrying a portable moviecamera. Kaufman was Dziga Vertov's cameraman.

Title page of *Soviet Cinema*, no. 4, 1927.

Cover for A. Latsis' and L. Keilin's *Children and the Cinema* [Deti i kino] ("Teakinopechat," 1928).

Cover for *The Results of the First Five-Year Plan* ("Partizdat," 1933).

Moskve sotsialisticheskoi]. The album included more than fifty photographs taken by Rodchenko, Alexander Savelev, Kazachinsky, Eleazar Langman, and Boris Ignatovich. The photos were printed horizontally on pages slightly longer than normal. The new and the old were placed side by side, so that aspects of both were simultaneously present in each separate sheet: the "respectable public" on Red Square in the 1900s and a sports parade in the 30s; "nanny with the young gentlemen," and kindergartens and crêches; reconstruction, widening the streets and squares. To the extent that the new cadres of "Socialist Moscow" dominate these pages, and that they, for the most part, reflect the Constructivist foreshortening and clarity typical of Soviet photography in the 30s, the whole publication acquires a precise and uniform visual effect. Used as it is here for the purposes of publicity, photo-art becomes the dominant means of expression and defines the album's character. The artist here would appear to be neutral, merely choosing his subjects with a view to contrasting the old and new, and through their arrangement, underlining and intensifying their inner dynamics and compositional structure.

The album *Ten Years of Uzbekistan* [10 let Uzbekistana] is an example of book design directed entirely by the artist, who uses a maximum of expressive possibilities in every aspect of the volume — from the case, the binding, and the title page to the presentation of the text and the quotations, the inclusion of ornamental decorative structures (both drawings and photos), and the printing of the photographs in shades of green, red, brown and blue. An article dated December 21, 1934 in the newspaper *Pravda*, entitled "A Marvellous Piece of Work," reads: "nor have the past few years been unproductive for the printing, design and publishing technology. To these examples we must unquestionably add the recently issued album *Ten Years of Uzbekistan*. This album has been richly and marvellously done! An orgy of colors intoxicates the gaze in the very best possible reproduction of the beauties of this naturally beautiful Soviet republic."

Turning to the first chapter, "Uzbekistan Today," we find most of the photos mounted one to a page. There are close-ups and general views; some of the photos run to the very edge of the page, others have borders. The artists have anticipated the composition of each shot; they seem to have envisioned the photo beforehand, just as it appears in the album. They have realized the frame's hidden potential for overcoming and going beyond the confines of the page. This is the kind of extremely complex problem which can only be solved by someone with unerring visual acumen.

The varied tonality and color of the images creates an impression of colored photographs: duplex printing in different shades makes for a more exciting presentation. The album's arrangement by subject matter is inseparable from its plastic structure — the sequence of colors, the cellophane bastard-titles, and the insets. The theme of Uzbekistan's development and progress is perceived through the juxtaposition of shots, the diversity of the montage, and the internal connectedness of the images.

Photomontage double-spreads from *The Results of the First Five- Year Plan*, 1932.

Cover for *From Merchant Moscow to Socialist Moscow* ("Ogiz-Izogiz," 1932).

Bindings and title page for Aseev's *Collected Poems in Four Volumes* [Sobranie stikhotvorenii v 4-kh tomakh] ("GIKhL," 1932).

Cover for Maiakovsky's *Menacing Laughter* [Groznyi smekh]
("GIKhL," 1932).

Stepanova in the editorial office of "Partizdat," 1932.

Fly-leaf of Maiakovsky's *Menacing Laughter*, 1932.

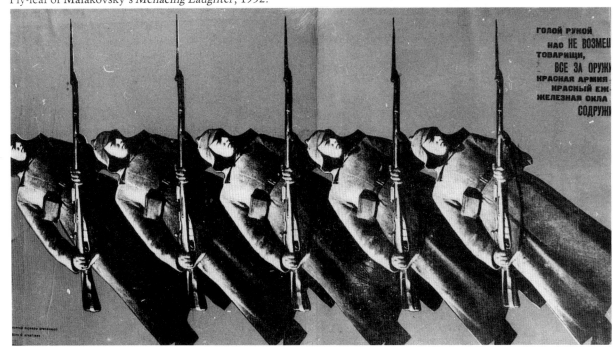

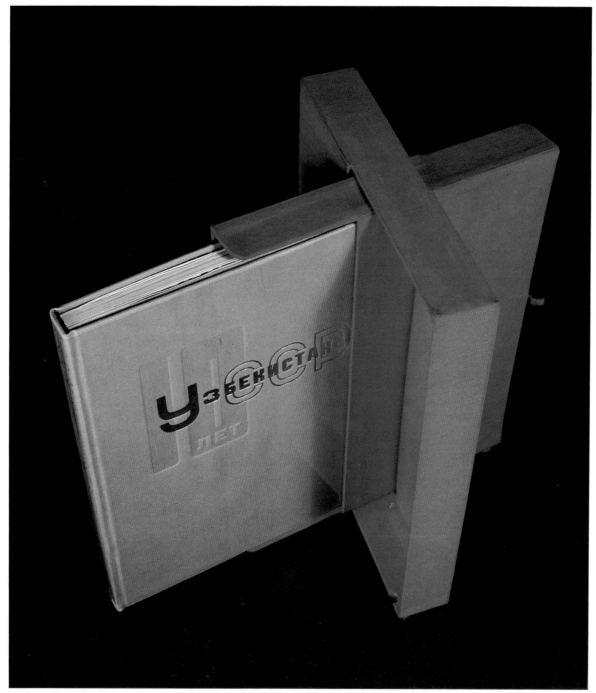

Rodchenko and Stepanova, alternative case and binding for *Ten Years of Uzbekistan* ("Ogiz-Izogiz," 1934).

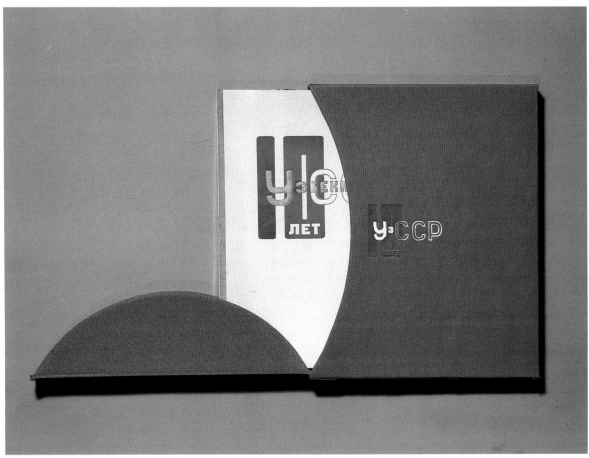

Rodchenko and Stepanova, binding and fly-leaf of *Ten Years of Uzbekistan*, 1934.

Double-spread from *Ten Years of Uzbekistan*, 1934.

Cover for *USSR Under Construction*, no. 8, 1936.

Rodchenko and Stepanova, double-spread from *USSR Under Construction*, no. 8, 1936.

Double-spread from *USSR Under Construction*, no. 8, 1936. The little pamphlet attached to the center of the spread contains information on exporting timber through sea ports.

Double-spread from *USSR Under Construction*, no. 8, 1936.

Double-spread from *USSR Under Construction*, no. 8, 1936.

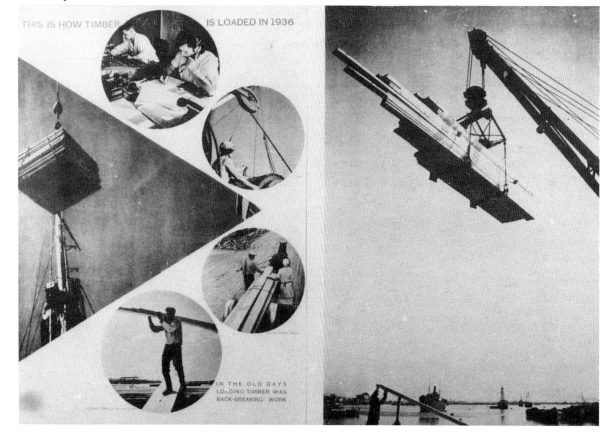

Cover for *USSR Under Construction*, no. 12, 1935.

Rodchenko and Stepanova, double-spread from *USSR Under Construction*, no. 12, 1935.

Double-spread from *USSR Under Construction*, no. 12, 1935.

Double-spread from *USSR Under Construction*, no. 12, 1935, with a folded paper parachute.

The same double-spread from *USSR Under Construction*, no. 12, 1935, with the parachute unfolded.

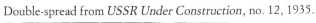

Double-spread from *USSR Under Construction*, no. 12, 1935.

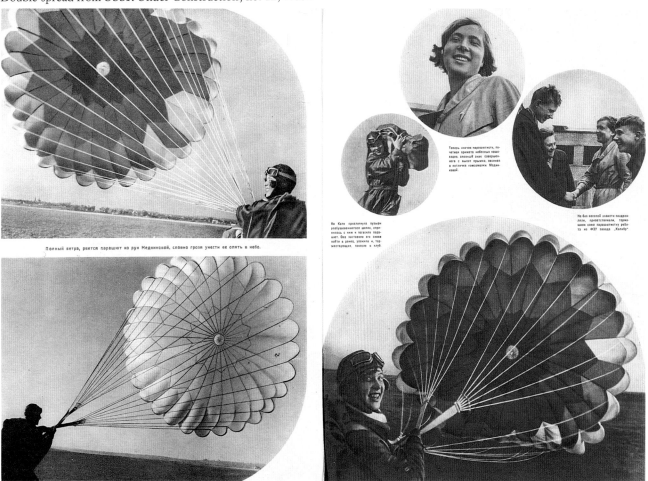

Rodchenko and Stepanova, case and binding for *The First Cavalry* ("Ogiz-Izogiz," 1938).

Double-spread title page for *The First Cavalry*, 1938.

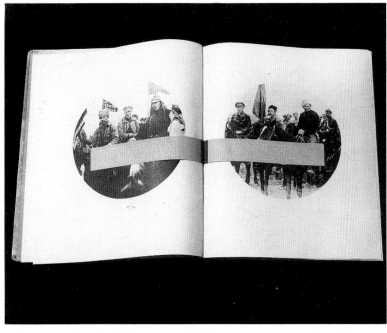

A second major section in the album is entitled "The Country and its People" (there were also sections on agriculture, industry and culture). It too is mostly photographic, but uses a different color scheme of ochres, greens and blues. Naturally, the juxtaposition and order of the colors is not arbitrary, but is strictly dictated by the requirements of the polygraphic process. Stepanova would always make a tiny maquette that simulated the order in which the printed pages and colored images would be sewn together.

In every element of the design of *Ten Years of Uzbekistan* one senses the artists' attention to the technological demands of the polygraphic process, their ability to apply it expressively and appropriately. They used not only a variety of printing methods (relief printing — duplex and polychrome, lithography, and intaglio printing), but also many different materials (chalk paper, lithographic paper, cellophane, gelophane). This was the first time that plastics were used in book design, a development that required particular attention to the judicious application of their peculiar qualities of transparency, malleability, and so on. The bindings were printed in several variants: the basic edition had printing and stamping on silk or bast matting, while a limited number of copies were bound in white celluloid stamped and printed in gold. Another distinctive feature of the album was its unusual, specially constructed vertical case, which consisted of a narrow spine connecting the two semicircular sides.

These experiments with bindings were not confined to the traditional materials of cardboard, leatherette, and fabric. In the experimental workshops at Izogiz (which specialized in one-of-a-kind presentation editions) cases were made of plexiglass, celluloid and even metal. Through the medium of the book Rodchenko and Stepanova succeeded yet again in demonstrating the breadth of thought and universality of the artist-constructor, their ability to find new and unusual ways to apply their inventiveness.

The number of the journal *USSR Under Construction* [SSSR na stroike] devoted to parachuting (no. 12, 1935), which Rodchenko and Stepanova designed, will long remain a unique example of how original constructive ideas can be applied to mass-produced typography. The leitmotif for the journal became a parachute and the way it operated by unfolding a flat form in space. It was not for nothing that a real parachute hung from the high ceiling in their studio, and that they studied each fold of the fabric. The idea of unfolding a flat surface, corresponding to the actual mechanics of a parachute, became part of the plastic structure of this issue of the journal. One had only to pull on the folded corners at specific points for the image to gradually reveal itself in several stages.

By way of comparison, let us turn to another Rodchenko and Stepanova issue of *USSR Under Construction* (no. 6, 1936) on lumber exports. The external treatment is calmer, the pages are scarcely transformed. The cover shows the beautiful pattern of a section of wood veneer, while the pages reproduce graphically the elegant texture of tree crowns, planks and logs. A small folded booklet with facts on the export of lumber is placed in the center of the spread, emphasizing the relationship of paper to the timber from which it is manufactured — a book within a book that gives a new metaphoric dimension to the journal's content. In a review of this issue, the English *Timber Trade Journal* called it a poem about timber.

We can see, then, how Rodchenko and Stepanova gave plastic expression to a particular subject-matter, how they found a visual or constructive principle inherent in the theme. Even without the finished photographs in hand, Rodchenko and Stepanova made unerring compositional schemes for each page, setting out the sequence of the spreads and the succession of close-ups and distant views. Using this constructive method it was possible to make swift and exact decisions on the structure of the book at the most basic compositional and geometric level, and to specify the type and character of the necessary frames, photomontages, and other graphic material. In this sense their work paralleled that of the film director and the scriptwriter, the only difference being that this film sometimes played simultaneously on both sides of the page at once. The artists became the coordinator of the publication, thanks to their elaboration of its compositional and structural bases.

Work on these photo-albums required that Rodchenko and Stepanova both visualize the graphic form and compositional structure of the image, and also project how a particular subject might develop over time. In other words, the composition of the photo-books, the albums, and the photo-journals on which they worked throughout the 30s was resolved not only through the use of all possible spatial coordinates, but also by taking into account the dynamics of an image's temporal development. This was clearly demonstrated in a purely historical artistic study — the photo-album called *The First Cavalry* [Pervaia konnaia].

Work on this album began in 1936 and the book was published the following year. Judging by Stepanova's memoirs, "How we Worked on *The First Cavalry*," the artists began work on the album from scratch. Not just the historical and visual material, but also all the documentary photographic material on the October Revolution and the Civil War had to be put together piece by piece. Rodchenko's personal photo-archive — the remains of a Moscow newspaper's archive that had been salvaged from a flooded basement in the 20s — came in handy as well. These unique shots of street battles, portraits of Red Army soldiers, and incidents involving the toppling of imperial monuments were also used by Rodchenko in posters (*The History of the All-Union Communist Party (of Bolsheviks)* [Istoriia VKP (b)], on the covers of books and journals (*To the Living Lenin* [Zhivomu Ilichy] and *LEF*), and in the political photomontages for the journal *Abroad* [Za rubezhom].

The First Cavalry presented these photo-documents in an entirely new light. Small, yellowing proofs of varying quality and size were blown up to full-page size (36 × 30 cm). The images were framed, wherever necessary a background of sky, ground or trees was added, and the photo-image was restored and adapted to the new format. In principle, thanks to such

Photomontage pages from *The First Cavalry*, 1938.

Case and alternative binding for *The First Cavalry*, 1938.

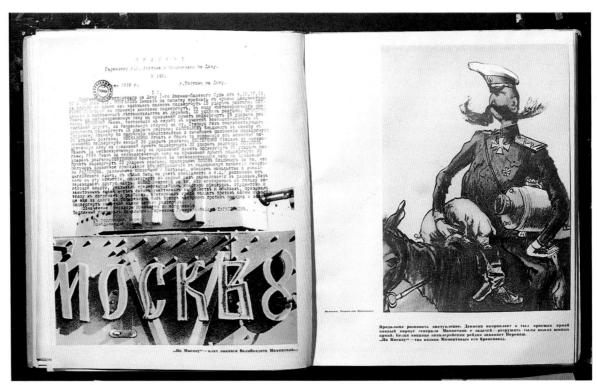

Photomontage double-spread from *The First Cavalry*, 1938.

Photomontage double-spread from *The First Cavalry*, 1938, including facsimile reproductions of documents inserted into the binding.

skillful and imperceptible mounting, a variety of compositions could be made from a single photo. For instance, by enlarging the foreground and adding it to a smaller print of the same photo, a visually deeper space could be created while still retaining the photo's historical flavor. The intricate combination of the young Semion Budenny's full-size portrait with a photo of the house where he was born, both sharing the same convincing optical perspective, created a completely new photo based on documentary images. These methods of covert photomontage which Stepanova employed increased the page's informational and illustrative capacity. The two artists' initial idea of creating a documentary album on the history of the First Cavalry found its artistic, plastic expression in the principles of constructing synthetic photo-images and in the application of actual contemporary documents.

On the first page of the March 9, 1918 issue of *Pravda*, along with a call to workers and peasants to join the Red Army, there was a photo of a column of Red Army men with rifles. On a sheet of the newspaper *Red Cavalryman* [Krasnyi kavalerist] for March 11, 1920, printed under the heading "The enemy front has been breached. Berdichev and Zhitomir occupied," was a photo of Red cavalrymen at full gallop. By merging the two documents — the newspaper and the image — a new piece of journalism was achieved that was both visually and emotionally expressive.

Probably only a poligraphic artist with a particular flair for the printing process could use every scrap of paper, every document of an epoch so skillfully and cleverly. Rodchenko and Stepanova found room in their album not only for posters from the Civil War period or for the Kukryniksy group's caricatures of White generals, but also for pages from Budenny's order book and a telegram from Mikhail Frunze on the liquidation of the Southern Front. A small flyer appealing to the Polish soldiers to halt their military activity against the Soviet Republic, a small poster by Maiakovsky from the ROSTA series — all such documents were reproduced in facsimile and glued between the pages of the album, thus transforming it into an archival folder in which the innumerable testaments of a heroic epoch were carefully collected and filed.

The principle of "bringing a document to life", as Stepanova calls it in her article, was practised with such care and tact that, leafing through the album, the reader scarcely notices the designer's presence. There are three hundred pages in the album, printed with great care in an Egyptian-style typeface. In the purely design elements of the album (the binding, case and bastard-titles), however, Rodchenko and Stepanova made no secret of their authorship. The binding and case are rather reminiscent of a commander's field case, an impression strengthened by the fact that the lid of the case has a photo of a mounted cavalryman with full ammunition.

Creating a photo-album differs from normal book design in the complexity and variety of the problems it raises, and also in the amount of time it takes. Collecting and classifying material becomes a complicated research project which only the artist is capable of carrying out in the context of the album. The con-

trols for *The First Cavalry* filled several folders with more than two thousand subjects, including documentary photos, posters and flyers, portraits, shots of horses, etc. The work took well over a year.

Stepanova and Rodchenko continued to work on the illustrated photographic book in their photo-album *The Red Army* [Krasnaia armiia], published in 1938 by Ogiz-Izogiz. Unlike *The First Cavalry* there were no synthetic photomontages, and everything was done with the utmost precision. The documentary photos were linked thematically on the page, and their size and multiple dimensions were determined by a strict modular principle. The shape of the five-point star became the motif that ran through the whole volume: one of the variants for the metal case took this form, and it came up again in the bastard titles. Using a photogram Stepanova and Rodchenko designed an ornamental motif of stars for the fly-leaf. In the end, however, they used a more mechanized type of ornament composed of small airplane and tank silhouettes repeated many times on photographic paper and then transferred in reverse, that is, in a negative image.

Most of the administrative work for the photo-albums of the 30s and 40s was done by Stepanova. She kept a detailed record of when materials were received, tried to keep to the deadlines for submitting sketches and preparing the originals, and it was she who took care of the actual mechanism of book publishing, seeing the text and illustrations through the editorial offices and the print shop. Having worked as art editor on journals such as *Soviet Cinema* (1926-28), *Book and Revolution* (1928), *Red Student Life* (1929), *Radio Listener* (1929), and *Soviet Woman* [Sovietskaia zhenshchina] (1946), she had an excellent understanding of the typographical and publishing industries.

Stepanova also found new solutions in her work on posters about writers in the 1950s for the Bureau of Visual Aids attached to the Committee on Cultural Enlightenment of the SNK RSFSR (Council of Peoples' Commissars of the RSFSR). Each poster took the form of a mini-album devoted to the works of Victor Hugo, Anton Chekhov, Nikolai Nekrasov, Maiakovsky and others. The style and composition of each sheet reflected the art of the writer concerned.

In the 50s a method of binding the pages of experimental maquettes with a wire coil became very popular in the Rodchenko-Stepanova household. Replacing the traditional spine, the shining spiral gave even the unfinished rough-draft maquette a high-tech look. The Ministry of Agriculture's publishing house persuaded their printing house to use this method in the mass circulation of a vegetable-seed catalog which Stepanova and Rodchenko designed in 1957. The resulting publication was unusually interesting thanks to the use of this streamlined, efficient effect.

The modern book designer's arsenal is amazingly varied, and it was Rodchenko and Stepanova who were among the first to demonstrate the wealth of artistic and expressive means possible in typography. These included spatial and volumetric methods of design, the graphic construction of an image and

Состязания продемонстрировали огромную работу, осуществленную в области конного дела.

The First Cavalry, 1938. Photomontage on the theme of "the cavalry today."

Rodchenko and Stepanova, alternative metal case for *The Red Army* ("Ogiz-Izogiz," 1938).

Bastard-title for *The Red Army*, 1938.

the contextual montage of information, the use of images as plastic metaphors, and the inclusion of photodocuments. The books that Stepanova and Rodchenko designed incorporated a good deal from their own projects in architecture, design and the theater. Their books are as socially relevant, expedient, constructive, and functional as Stepanova's clothing and fabric designs or Rodchenko's designs for furniture and light fixtures. Their work with theater posters and advertisements, and their involvement in cultural and educational establishments trained them to work with vivid colors and on a large scale. Photography fostered attention to the value of documentary truth and a special feel for the frame. Photomontage revealed the importance of metaphors in book design. Leaflets, trademarks, bookmarks and packaging, all trained their powers of invention and imagination in both the overall treatment and the details of type-face composition. They were designers in the very broadest sense of the word. Rodchenko spoke the truth when he asserted that "the man who organizes his life, his work, and himself, is a modern artist."

СТРАНА СОВЕТОВ НА-ЧЕКУ

Photomontage page from *The Red Army*, 1938.

Alternative fly-leaf for *The Red Army*, 1938.
Fly-leaf from *The Red Army*, 1938. Photogram.

Stepanova at her desk, 1932. Photo Alexander Rodchenko.

Rodchenko and Stepanova, double-spread from *The USSR Under Construction*, no. 7, 1940; issue on Maiakovsky.

Cover for *USSR Under Construction*, no. 7, 1940.

Cover for *Poligraphic Production* [Poligraficheskoe proizvodstvo], nos. 3-4, 1946.

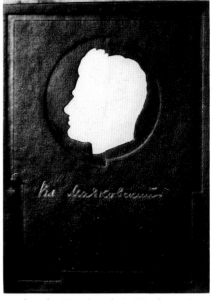

Binding for Maiakovsky's *Works in One Volume* [Sochineniia v odnom tome] ("GIKHL," 1940).

Rodchenko and Stepanova, binding for *Twenty-five Years of the Kazakh SSR* (Kazogiz [Kazakh Publishing house of the Visual Arts], 1945).

Rodchenko and Stepanova, transparent plexiglass cover and binding
for *The Cine-art of Our Motherland*, 1945 (unpublished).

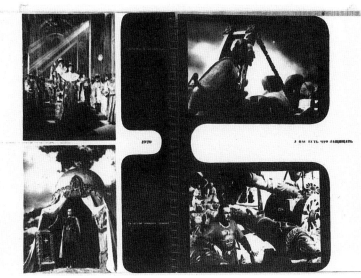

Double-spread from *The Cine-art of Our Motherland*, 1945.

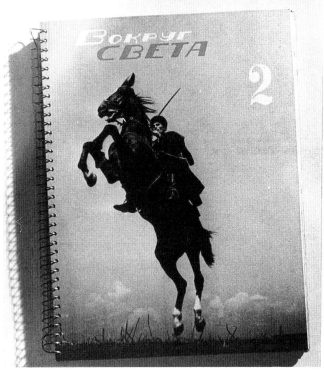

Lay-out design for *Around the World* [Vokrug sveta], 1946.

Title page from *The Cine-art of Our Motherland*, 1945.

Lay-out design for *Soviet Woman*, 1946.

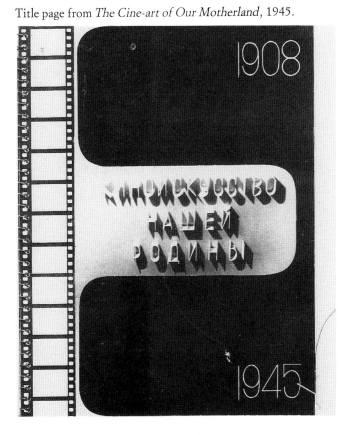

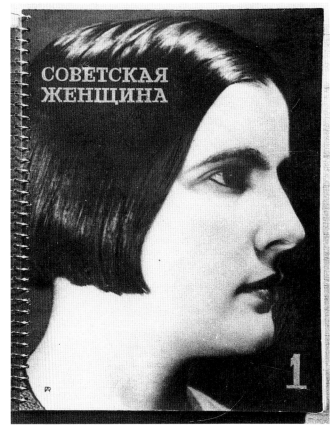

Kirov Street. Demonstration on November 7, 1939. Oil on cardboard, 42 × 31.

Asters, 1938. Oil on cardboard, 53.5 × 37.

Stepanova sketching, 1949. Photo Nikolai Lavrentiev.

Seventeen years after the "5 × 5 = 25" exhibition of 1921, Stepanova went back to painting. This return was typical of many artists of the Russian avant-garde. Malevich and Tatlin also returned to figurative painting, and in 1935 Rodchenko went back to his easel and began his circular compositions.

For Stepanova, it was as if she was learning to see and feel the world again. Rodchenko set up delicate still lifes selected according to a precise theme. High old stools and a round table were useful for this. Stepanova painted for hours on end, and sometimes the colors would even begin to fade. The brushstrokes were applied thick and put one in mind of a brick stack with their regular, uniform shape. In still lifes of vegetables, china and fruit, even dried fish with green onions, everything was selected according to color in order to create a specific color scale. Sometimes Stepanova painted still lifes under electric light, and then her canvases took on a warm yellowish tone. Sometimes she would take off her glasses (she was short-sighted) and paint flickering color patches of muffled, indistinct outlines. In landscape painting she loved to take a high viewpoint. From her balcony she would paint a demonstration far away on Kirov Street or a cityscape with a dirigible floating in the sky above. From the windows of a friend's apartment on the Arbat she painted Arbat Square with its passers-by and the old pre-war trollybuses.

Stepanova painted village and country landscapes in the area around Moscow, some of them at the end of the 30s before the Second World War, some in the late 40s when her daughter Varvara, a graduate of the Moscow Polygraphic Institute, would accompany her on sketching expeditions. They would paint the river, the bushes, the gullies, while alongside them Varvara's husband Nikolai Lavrentiev, also a book designer, was busy with his camera. He picked up where Rodchenko left off, in chronicling the family, photographing guests, the studio, and Stepanova working.

Stepanova painted her sketches in oil on cardboard. Each stroke was laid down like a tiny fragment of colored mosaic and has its own nuance. Where several strokes come together the paint stands up in peaks, so that the surface of the sketch vibrates not only with color but also with light and shade. It feels sharp and rough to the touch. At a distance you sense its vibration through the air and that all the objects are as one.

Rodchenko painted the circus as a poetic metaphor of life, out of a need to create his own unified and complete world on canvas. He worked from memory and imagination. Stepanova worked from life, but by means of color she too constructed a new world. Perhaps in painting she attempted to accomplish that which had become so difficult to accomplish in design.

Moscow. View from a Window with a Dirigible, 1938. Oil on cardboard, 36.5 × 53.5.

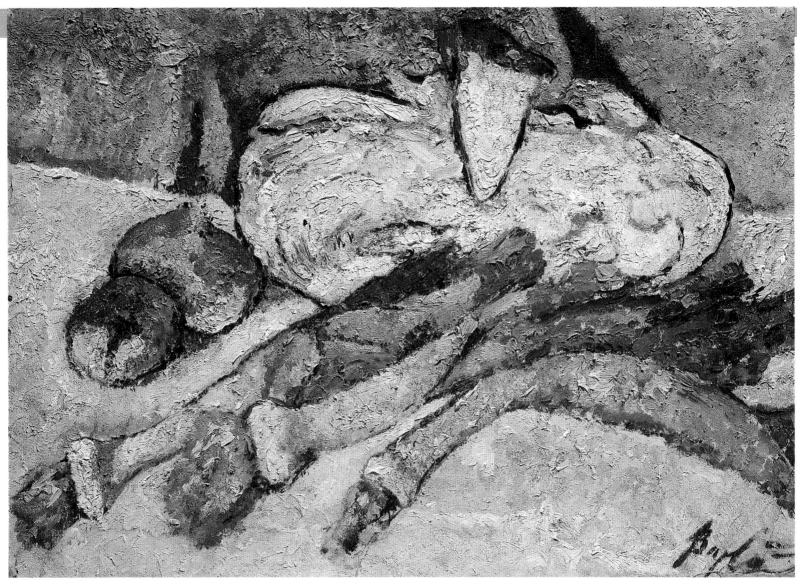

Cabbage and Onions, 1939. Oil on cardboard, 36.5 × 53.5.

Stepanova with her daughter Varvara at Kallistovo (near Moscow), 1950. Photo Nikolai Lavrentiev.

Stepanova and S. S. Lavrentiev at Kallistovo, 1950. Photo by Nikolai Lavrentiev.

Still Life with Apples, 1938. Oil on cardboard, 36.5 × 53.5.

The Blue Teapot, 1939. Oil on cardboard, 54 × 36.

Stepanova at work on a maquette for *Moscow Under Reconstruction*, 1938.

In temperament, Rodchenko and Stepanova were totally different. Rodchenko was calm and took his time about things. When he spoke it was always with a half-smile on his face. Nothing ever seemed to make him angry . . . unless it was something that hindered him from working. He was always thinking about something, a frown wrinkling his forehead into four horizontal creases . . . . He loved people, and scarcely a day passed without visitors dropping by. Stepanova was short, energetic and smiling. Her voice was loud and earnest. She seemed to be Rodchenko's complement, his second half. Together they formed a single image, born of many years of collective and constant creativity. They were a family of artists, with the second generation myself and my husband Nikolai Lavrentiev, whom I met as a student at the Moscow Polygraphic Institute. I began my studies there in 1943. Our first assignment was to sketch a book cover on the subject of the circus. Father told me that I should begin on a small scale and just map out the general construction and outline, being sure to make several variants. The second stage was to select the sketches and scale them up to the required size.

Almost any of the alternative ideas Rodchenko came up with might be the key one, since he worked in stylistic series. But sometimes he would devise sketches that were stylistically very different, as if two or three different artists had designed them. Pencil in hand, he could map out a scheme on any theme. A clear mental image of the type-face block, or of the composition of the type-face and the image, would materialize.

From 1932 on, Stepanova and Rodchenko worked for many years on photo-albums. Why did this type of book attract them? Publishing houses produced various kinds of photo-album, but Rodchenko and Stepanova came up with a range of new types: the simple album-folder, the complex album filled with information, the large-format album, the presentation album.

In most cases Stepanova and Rodchenko determined the size of a publication by making mock-ups. During work on the album *The First Cavalry*, for instance, they made three different sizes of block. The blocks were prepared at the printing-house with a number of variant designs on the sides. Rodchenko and Stepanova introduced the practise of reducing or enlarging the size of the page to emphasize the subject matter.

Rodchenko designed a variety of cases for these photo-albums in the shape of a square, semicircle, star, triangle, and so on. They could be slid apart, compacted for more convenient use on a table, or folded for storage on the shelf.

What little text there is was written afterwards. First of all the visual text was created out of photographs. But who decided exactly what would be featured in a photo-album? Only an artist can do this, by working with the visual images like a type-setter, laboriously fitting word to word, arranging a phrase out of separate photos.

In the course of more than a decade Stepanova worked with many master photographers. Georgii Petrusov and Ivan Shagin worked with her on the albums *Moscow* and *The Moscow*

(*left to right*) V. Kinelovsky, G. Fish, and Stepanova, 1950. Photo Nikolai Lavrentiev.

Stepanova in her studio, 1948. Photo V. Kovrigin.

Metro (published by Izogiz), photographing the architecture of the Moscow streets, the cars, and the people. But though the scenario of *Moscow* was completed, and the montage sheets for the double-spreads pasted up, it was never published.

The same subject was photographed many times, the final shot which the artist selected being the one that seemed most suitable in theme, lighting and composition. The photo was then placed in its slot alongside the other picture-words. Close-ups were alternated with general shots, details, and a single series of visual images. As in speech, there were rhythms and pauses, "sentences" and "adjectives," all the nuances of photographic meaning.

In addition to composing albums from pre-existing photographs, Stepanova also looked for ways to use photography as an element in design. For this she required very precisely executed, technically "pure" images of objects, and so she often worked with Khlebnikov, a master of the applied technical photograph. Among the complicated assignments he worked on were still lifes, stacks of opened books, cut-out paper figures, a variety of textured backgrounds, wooden boards, paper, and scattered seeds. For the album *Five Years of the Labor Reservists* [5 let trudovykh reservov], Khlebnikov took exposures of Russian wood carving and *naboika*, and the light tonal patterns that resulted were used to decorate the pages of the album.

For an issue of *USSR Under Construction* on the subject of the elections to the Supreme Soviet of the USSR, Rodchenko photographed garlands of artificial roses intertwined, as it were, with the text on the page.

Rodchenko and Stepanova used both "visible" and "invisible" photomontage. In visible photomontage two or more photos were merged by printing or gluing them together, overprinting documents, charts, and so on. "Invisible" photomontage involved improving the general appearance of a single photo which was in poor condition but which contained essential data. So, for example, by overprinting a beautiful sky with clouds, the photograph became visually more interesting. Photos could also be improved by framing and eliminating unwanted parts. The actual shape of the photo could also be changed to a circle, oval, square, etc.

How did Stepanova and Rodchenko work? The preliminary sketches that Rodchenko produced served as the first clue, just the faintest image of what a book, a cover, or an album might look like. Stepanova would then work up this idea using all available polygraphic resources. After this came a group decision on page lay-out. Rodchenko had an excellent grasp of how photographic material could be placed and grouped within the frame and the rectangle of the page. The size of each photo, the shape of its frame, and its exact position in the margin was calculated. Rodchenko and Stepanova worked with books as if they were conductors, manipulating an orchestra of color and photo-images that rhythmically resonated against each other, allowing the reader to assimilate the work in its entirety. In Stepanova's accurate, day-to-day record of the progress of their commissioned works, her notes are brief, as if they had been made by a "robot" secretary.

Stepanova's work table stood opposite the studio window. She sat facing the window, bending forward slightly on her white stool. A lamp with a green shade, brushes in a glass. A T-square, bottles of paint, a drafting set. All these things still sit on this table. She wore glasses, but when working she would rest them on her forehead. She worked mostly at night, wearing a dressing-gown and bedroom slippers, a cigarette in her mouth. Someone would call through an order and the "ignition" would start up. Once Stepanova had entered the client's name in the work book, she would begin to familiarize herself with the scope of the publication, and select the material, the outline, and the composition for the covers. The plans were then carried out in color, and a balance of black and white chosen. Alternatives were selected. Some parts were enlarged, others elaborated. The sketches were scaled up to full size.

Their days were so taken up with these publications that even now, forty years later, as I read their hurried notes, I see the day's work, an order for a publication and its execution all summed up in a single swift line.

In the difficult post-war years up to 1948 Stepanova sewed and knitted warm clothing for herself. As a young girl she had worked in a seamstress's shop, and she crocheted a set of clothes out of multicolored wools, using every scrap of woollen yarn in the house. She designed an open-work net ground in black, through which she threaded different colored wools. The result was a thick, warm jacket with pockets. She also crocheted hats with stripes like ribbons around the brim. My father would say jokingly: "The Varvarshvei Spinning Trust is open." In a photo of 1920 Rodchenko is wearing production clothing sewn by Stepanova, in which the stitched seams, pockets, collar and cuffs are delineated by leather detailing.

The specific requirements of a photo-album are complex, and the artist-designer must wear several hats. Though logically speaking it is the author who should work first with the material, in most cases that work lacks sufficient attention to detail. Stepanova, therefore, would often work out the plan and the text for the albums without even an exact title. She started from nothing, as happened for instance with *The First Cavalry*, in which she figured as co-author of the text. The same was true of *The Cine-art of Our Motherland*. Initially the plan and the text were to have been done by Shklovsky, but he refused because he was too busy. The job was then given to Eisenshtein's wife, Pera Atasheva who, together with Stepanova, prepared the text for the album.

Frequently work was held up by difficulties in obtaining materials, a common problem in those days. There was no paper and cardboard on sale to make the maquettes, no glue, no leatherette for binding, etc. Even dextrine glue could not be bought, and they had to ask their clients to get it for them. Often in Stepanova's notebooks I came across phrases such as: "Went to the warehouse, took some samples of silk and leather .... They delivered some plexiglass but not the size we ordered .... Kolia drove to the printing-house for glue."

The final demonstration model to be shown to the publishing house was beautifully worked out right down to the last detail. The dust-jacket was glued on cardboard, the text written out, the binding made with typographic printing, and the montages for the page lay-out made from actual color photographs. All this was sewn together in a block and either stitched or spiral-bound.

Some of their ideas for designing albums were inspired by the textures of a particular material. In the unpublished album *The Central Museum of V. I. Lenin* [Tsentralnyi muzei V. I. Lenina], for instance, Rodchenko and Stepanova wanted the names of the Museum's halls to be printed on a marble ground. But they found that the veining in real marble was too indistinct and undefined, and when a real piece of marble was photographed, the gray background lacked expression. So Rodchenko made an experiment. He submerged the photopaper in a waterbath to which he had added some drops of oil paint. The paint adhered to the paper in thread-like patterns that imitated marble veining.

Again, for the title page of an album on visual resources called *In the World of the Invisible* [V mire nevidimykh] (published by Sovetskaia Rossiia in 1960, initially under the title *Microbes*), they photographed a round convex lense to represent a drop of water under the microscope. On top of the photograph they superimposed a drawing of bacteria to create the illusion of a magnified drop, with the glass creating the effect of volume and the patch of light. On the album cover they showed the changes in light across the surface of the circle, as if one was looking through the eye-piece of a microscope. The original maquettes were made in light for a polychrome offset.

But by this stage, in 1958, Varvara Fedorovna was already seriously ill in hospital. And so it was I who prepared the originals and brought the plates to the publishing house.

Varvara Rodchenko, 1984

Stepanova in her studio, 1950. Photo Nikolai Lavrentiev.

Stepanova with her grandson Alexander (the author), 1956. Photo Nikolai Lavrentiev.

Nikolai Lavrentiev and Varvara Rodchenko, 1947. Photo Alexander Rodchenko.

Stepanova on the balcony, 1925. Photo Alexander Rodchenko.

In his photos of the mid-1920s, Rodchenko often used Stepanova as a prototype image for his montages, writing on the negatives: "Varvara with her eyes wide open," "Messenger," "Komsomol girl in a headscarf," "Book-pedlar." The photo had to be staged with theatrical exaggeration, pointed and symbolic. Stepanova would vamp for Rodchenko and think up outlandish costumes and hairstyles. She could transform herself as skillfully as a professional actress on the silent screen.

Thanks to Rodchenko's photos we can see Stepanova at work on a great variety of projects throughout her creative life. They range from the maquettes for *The Death of Tarelkin* to fabric design, from the imposition of journals to the glueing of book originals. Stepanova's desk was always piled with projects the two of them were working on. But Rodchenko found time to record not just "production" portraits, but lyrical portraits as well. Sometimes Stepanova would be stylized "à la française" (after Rodchenko's trip to Paris in 1925) or as a serious "lady," as a frenzied Constructivist or an impassioned Komsomol girl. In the 1910s Rodchenko and Stepanova had used poetry as a vehicle for their declarations of love: in 1924 the language of love became photography. Stepanova was the subject of many of Rodchenko's photographic methods: double exposure with superimposed images, shooting against the light, contrasting light and shade, the use of foreshortening. The image of Stepanova the individual, her psychological states, her unique personality, emerges from this mass of documentary and artistic photographs. The portraits distributed throughout this book help to recreate Stepanova's creative environment.

Stepanova with her daughter Varvara, 1950. Photo Nikolai Lavrentiev. On the wall are paintings by Stepanova and Rodchenko from the 1930s and 1940s.

Stepanova. An experiment in illuminating the face through fabric, 1928. Photo Alexander Rodchenko.

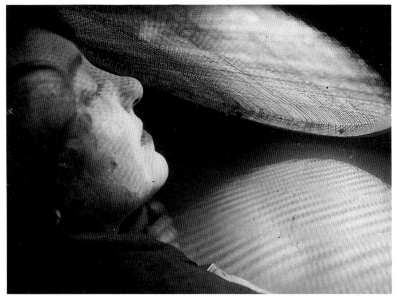

Students of VKhUTEMAS in the studio of Rodchenko and Stepanova. Core members of the study sub-group "The Group of INKhUK Constructivists:" A. I. Akhtyrko, I. K. Morozov, Z. N. Bykov, Stepanova, P. K. Zhigunov.

Stepanova with beads, in an armchair, 1928. Photo Alexander Rodchenko.

Stepanova with a cigarette and "Dobrolet" badge, 1924. Photo Alexander Rodchenko.

Stepanova wearing a hat, 1924. Photo Alexander Rodchenko.

(*left to right*) V. Kukushkin, Stepanova, N. Pertsova, V. Pertsov (literary critic and author of a book on Maiakovsky), and Rodchenko, 1954. Photo Nikolai Lavrentiev.

Stepanova. Double exposure. 1924. Photo Alexander Rodchenko.

Stepanova with a cigarette, 1924. Photo Alexander Rochenko.

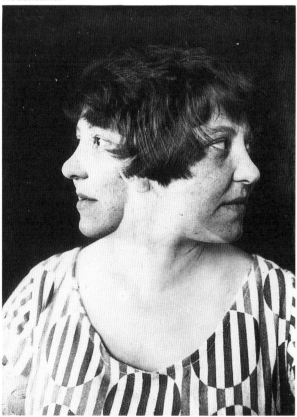

Stepanova in a hat, 1936. Photo Alexander Rodchenko.

Non-objective Creativity

The phase which followed Cubo-Futurism in the movement of art throughout the world began with non-objective art, a phenomenon which should be regarded not merely as a trend in painting, but as a new world view encompassing every aspect of art and life. This movement was a protest of the spirit against the materialism of modern life, and painters were among the first to perceive it. Incidentally, I should point out that painting is beginning to occupy an increasingly large place in world culture, despite all the "prayers for the dying" which the "born critics" are intoning over it.

The first slogans of non-objective creativity were proclaimed in 1913. From its very inception non-objective creativity has advanced by way of analysis and, being a young movement, has not as yet demonstrated its synthesis. This is why it is of value in this present time of terrible crisis, when art has lost its old traditions and is on the verge of falling into academicism for the sake of creating a new synthesis. It is not synthesis that reveals new paths, however, but analysis and invention.

In tracing the process of non-objective art in painting, we find two factors, one spiritual (the battle against the object and "representation" in the cause of free creativity and proclaimed acts of creation and inventiveness), the other concerned with expanding the professional demands of painting. Once the literary subject matter was lost, non-objective painters were obliged to improve the quality of execution, something which their predecessors were frequently saved from doing by the subject matter of the painting. Great, I would even say scientific, professional demands began to be made of the painter, in matters of facture, craftsmanship and technique, matters which in non-objective art place the painting high on the pedestal of painterly culture.

For now, the non-objective painters are united within a caste which their painterly principles have purged of dilettantes and the semi-educated.

Of course, the average "cultured" viewer whose comprehension of new achievements is slow in evolving, finds it difficult to keep up with the changes made by the non-objectivists as they advance along the revolutionary path of new discoveries, leaving in their wake the past stages of Futurism and Cubism. But if we accept "continuity" as an axiom, then non-objective creativity is the logical and legitimate outcome of the preceding stages in the creation of painting. However, that same viewer, not being corrupted by subject matter in a painting and not being so "cultured" that he demands representation everywhere and always in art, should understand this creativity with his feelings and his unspoiled intuition as a new beauty, a beauty of disruption, a beauty born of painting's liberation from centuries of accursed subject matter and the depiction of what is visible.

In non-objective creativity you won't find anything "familiar" or "comprehensible," but don't let this exasperate you, come to love art, grow to understand the tenet "to live for art," don't just study it and learn to discriminate, to look for subject matter that you understand, the representation of themes you may wish for.

As yet non-objective creativity is just the dawning of a great new epoch, of a time of great creativity hitherto unseen, destined to open the doors to mysteries more profound than science and technology.

It should be noted in passing that non-objective creativity has not created its own doctrinaire system and perhaps, in contrast to its predecessors, never will. It contains a thousand possibilities and great freedom for newer and newer achievements.

For the catalog of the 10th State Exhibition
1918

Two Figures, 1920. Oil on canvas, 70.5 × 56.

Following its logical development painting has now arrived at non-objectivity.

Not so long ago the slogan "Art as an end in itself" was rejected even by the defenders of "easel painting" — that is, painting of a specific size, painting as something narrowly professional, painting and only painting, without meaning or spiritual aspiration. This is the painting of synthesis — monumental painting — which is an essential index . . . . But painting advances not through synthesis but through analysis and innovation, something that is always extreme but that provides stimulus and subsequent progression.

Non-objective creativity is a movement of the spirit, a protest against the narrow materialism and naturalism that have begun to dominate life. Non-objective creativity is a new approach to every sphere of life and art. The first to be aware of it were painters. In recent times, it should be noted, painting has begun to occupy a dominant place in the universal movement. Among the other arts painting has decidedly gone furthest in its development and achievements . . . .

The period of transition that preceded non-objectivity in Russia produced painters who were able to extrapolate a good deal from nature — not the essence, however, but the exterior of objects, their facture and interrelationship. This distracted them from the object as such. The difference between [these Russian painters] and French painting is enormous. Take Cubism . . . French Cubism takes the object, breaks it apart, makes selections, thinks it through, and on an absolutely defined plane surface gives you a picture-object, where this object, being utilized by painting, presents its best side and lives to its fullest potential.

The French learned from the object, but most Russian painters of this transitional period learned not from the object itself, but from French paintings of that object. Russian Cubism was concerned with elaborating space, not the object. They understood "breaking apart the object" in abstract terms and rejected the object of the picture in favor of painting.

In "Russian Cubist" paintings color played an important part, and it is the color of the paint that led artists away from Cubism. Investigations into the realm of color were undertaken and the object was renounced.

The shift towards the non-objective among Russian artists took place in approximately 1913. Around this time the slogan "easel painting" was coined, thereby bringing the transitional period to a close, as I mentioned above, and bringing the achievements of the past to their ultimate limit.

Initially, non-objective creativity was understood by each artistic individual differently: some conducted research in color, others in facture or composition. However, one group in particular has been prominent in its expansion and consciousness of non-objective creativity, and has posited a method or system for expressing non-objective painting. This primary method was Suprematism, and it was investigated in two ways: as the achievement of a new form (the square) and as the intensification of painting through color, which was to perform the role of "the new renaissance of painting."

The square is not a discovery, of course, but simply the ultimate logical progression of the cube. Color played a role in that it required the form of the square for optimal manifestation. Consequently, the impetus for painting's liberation from the object has been color, while the square has been its synthesis.

The Suprematists extolled the square plane of color which they began to develop and synthesize into a picture. They did not produce a further shift in the Suprematist canon, since color, which is the vital force of Suprematism, became subordinated to the square which occupied the dominant position.

What then did they discover? Suprematist compositions executed in embroidery, where the color is purer than that of pigments applied to canvas, or rendered from any kind of planes dyed in the very best method, began to compete with the painted canvas, and very successfully too. It is clear that Suprematism in its pure form is decorative and should have been applied as a new style, an amazing, powerful style. Perhaps Suprematism ought to have found a more advanced technical medium than painting with pigments on canvas, in order to take the Suprematist method to its ultimate conclusion. Suprematism has still not reached its full potential in painting. In the course of painting a picture paint at least three times more intense than is now available would have to be used in order for the color not to lose more than a fifth of its qualities.

However, the group of painters who at one time shared the method of Suprematism in non-objective art broke with those individuals who either sacrificed color to composition and painting (Udaltsova) or, conversely, intensified it to the point of being decorative and dissonant (Rozanova), and who finally abandoned the Suprematist method.

Such was the attempt to instill non-objective creativity into the system of Suprematism. Simultaneously, non-objective creativity also developed outside the methods of Suprematism, but here each individual artist found his own path without attempting to confine his inventiveness within a system (Rodchenko, Kandinsky) and without attaching any "ism" to his achievements. In general then, non-objective creativity in painting is at the first stage of its development, and it is difficult to single out an "ism" capable of characterizing it completely. There is, however, one pronounced trait evident in non-objective painting — a diversified treatment of the art of painting, and each artist's strong individual coloring — the possibility that each one of them will go on to create a school of his own.

The non-objectivists are on the move — toward inventiveness, analysis in the creation of painting, the painting of color (colorpainting), acuity of composition, the construction of a monotone painting (Drevin).

A more detailed discussion of each of the Non-Objectivists would only be possible in separate articles, since their art is individual and diverse in the extreme.

Varst
1919

"In its time almost every thing that forms part of the positive sciences has been rejected."

Camille Flammarion

Absolute and ceaseless movement foward is the vital and legitimate justification for the existence of art.

Art strives to penetrate the future, not return to the past.

It makes the work of art a "miracle," that is incomprehensible. It forces the viewer to discover the incomprehensible, to cognize art.

Man cannot live without a miracle. By nature he is fully alive when he is inventing, discovering, experimenting. The process of discovering a miracle, i.e. the incomprehensible, of unmasking, provides a motive for his spiritual activity, whether it manifests itself as thinking, as building a construction, or simply as organizing one's private life.

The more the incomprehensible is present in art, the more active it is, the less utilitarian it becomes in the literal sense and the more so in the figurative sense, as an impetus to creativity.

Materialism fundamentally undermines the idealist worldview (one that is sufficiently one-sided). But . . . for the time being the world exists and man lives. This is "a miracle," the incomprehensible, because we have not solved the question of why it exists. Perhaps later on we will be in a position to understand or unmask our spiritual life as we are now doing with our material life, but it cannot be denied that the latter exists because we do not know it, we cannot reveal it.

We cry, "down with aesthetics and taste," although both have already been discredited enough. But, of course, that is not everything, and form alone cannot be and is not the content of art. It is still not discovery.

The formal approach which people are now seeking in art is a tribute to the materialism of our time. Actually, none of us is ever guided by mathematics when we create. I do not subscribe to the idea that in painting, or even in a general way, every artist first sets himself a task and then paints it. We have not yet discovered the initial moment, or more precisely the incentive to creativity, otherwise we would not still be talking about "emotional and spontaneous creativity."

If, over recent years, these words have sometimes seemed inapplicable to a number of works, the reason lies in the fact that the technique of painting has made significant advances while not abandoning creativity.

Sustained work is essential in art, but . . . that alone does not make a work of art, for it lacks the incomprehensible, which through technical improvements, can now be manifested more clearly and precisely.

Exact knowledge is not enough to make one an inventor, whose imagination and technical skills allow him to realize his work, his invention, the incomprehensible. . . .

Only after he has established a concrete fact does the scientist discover the laws governing his discovery, that is only then can he explain it.

A work of art, like an invention, contains only what is truly real, and exact knowledge can add nothing. It is incomprehens-

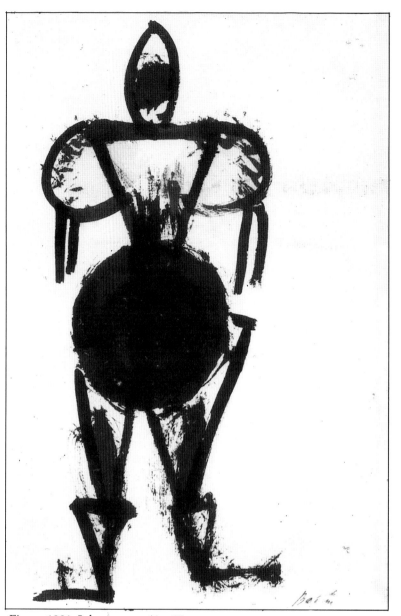

Figure, 1921. Ink on paper, 41 × 29.

ible (a miracle), or was incomprehensible (a miracle) if already unmasked, explored.

In a work of art a miracle, the incomprehensible, ought to exist both at the moment of creation and in its technical execution. In its formal execution it strives to be just as incomprehensible as it was at the first creative moment of its conception.

The painter of today knows no bounds to his impetuous desire to comprehend and master painterly technique.

He is penetrating the very essence of painting. He is beginning to know his own craftsmanship. Certainly, when compared to the future, this is just a first attempt. But the seriousness and consciousness which is evident in his work lead us to hope that a great deal will be revealed in the very near future.

1920

Active action. Production. The invention of a new, concrete object. Expedient organization.

An organism that is completely new in form can only be created through construction, existing for the physical realization of a specific goal.

So construction is not an end in itself. For this reason it is absurd to elevate construction into a goal or a new phase in art.

Construction excludes all aesthetics and taste, being based on technical necessity. One may assign oneself a task of construction and resolve it, i.e. solve it in one way or another, but it is impossible to produce from it a new content in painting. It may reflect the problems of modern life, but such an experiment is the result of various elements in the painting and the work of art. Even when working on a purely painterly problem, any solution that relies on artistic form (and hence on the aesthetic perception of a given form) will produce an element of vague confusion, a mixture of picture and experiment that is only an attempt at creating a new aesthetic.

Confining the use of material to the coefficient of extensibility does not in itself exhaust the possibilities of construction. It is in construction more than anywhere else that the question of making an object, of creating a new organism, is made clear.

From this it follows that construction is not 1) just the use of material or 2) a system of linking together separate parts, but rather a plan for carrying out a specific goal while observing both of these conditions.

The simple creation of an object (i.e. a utilitarian approach to the question) is not equivalent to construction, which requires expediency.

Why do we speak specifically of the construction, rather than the simple making, of an object? The object which is not made constructively is worse than one which is completely unmade, since it promotes the false impression that work is unskilled labor rather than organized, expedient and skilled activity.

A badly made object harms technolgy and engenders an approach to that object based on taste, expressed as an attempt to decorate it in some way that balances out its technical inadequacies. The constructive execution of a given object is replaced by taste and aesthetics.

The prettiness of an object almost always obstructs its significance and expediency.

A mark of constructiveness is the organic way in which its constituent parts are linked together. Even the most insignificant change in any of the parts leads to the destruction of the entire construction.

Another organism may be constructed anew out of the remaining parts, but they cannot be used for another task without a fundamental change in their meaning.

1920

A painting is a combination of idea and material through the process of artistic form. This latter element [artistic form] occupies the most important place in the artist's creative process, and is based on the fundamental distinction between practical life and creative abstraction. This abstraction has two aspects:

1. The spiritual (idea), as containing the realization of an ideal which does not exist in life, and which reflects the disintegration and rupture that has occured in life between work and play.

2. The material recording of the external form of the world — of the beauty of a given epoch, and of the excitement of living — by way of a painstaking perception of our experience of what exists. . . .

Aesthetic form exists only because it is divorced from life (Arvatov).

The false view that, in studying or becoming familiar with something, particularly with art, one must move in logical sequence from the simple to the complex, is based on a contemplative world view. Perhaps the roots run even deeper, since within such a system some people who are specialists in their field acquire a halo of knowledge. One man knows and won't tell all he knows straight away in case the spell is broken. When, finally, he reveals all that he knows it means he stands exposed. What he will do after that he doesn't know.

By relinquishing his knowledge gradually he holds the consumer in a state of spiritual dependency. He is someone who subjectively knows the individual development of his own knowledge, but who doesn't see the element of collective creativity that comes of working with a group of individuals.

Hence he misleads people by mixing up history and scientific knowledge.

After all it would be an obvious absurdity to study the technology of steam-engine construction as it originally existed in the nineteenth century. Clearly it is more expedient to use this time to be able to make something, even the smallest part of it, even a mere nut, if it can be put to use today.

In art just as in science there is no difference between physical, intellectual and technical production.

The present day is proceeding under the banner of "construction." We admire steam-engines and machines, and must not close our eyes to that fact. It is not correct that the Futurists select only moving parts in industrial culture, a reproach that is sometimes brought against us. This is merely an attempt to explain the decadence of our aspirations.

I think that the reason a steam-engine attracts one's attention more than any of the other objects and instruments of production is because, on the one hand, in its external appearance and in its goals it represents a completely finished construction, while, on the other, it is part and parcel of our everyday lives.

Regardless of which machine we select, it always has one drawback: the disparity between the machine and the environment in which it functions. The engineering profession which builds bridges and machines has still not managed to create a factory building. And we, as artists who have not yet transformed ourselves into organizers, cannot suddenly destroy our cultivated view of external form or our impulse to get an immediate sense of the entire building, the whole structure. It is natural, therefore, that we are drawn to, and feel most familiar with, that which has been concisely formulated and is totally integrated.

V. Toporkov's approach [a critic who wrote *Everyday Technology and Contemporary Art* (Teknicheskii byt i sovremennoe iskusstvo), 1928] to the machine in terms of understanding its technical form is correct. But all that he has to say about its artistic form is based on the old approach to art that involves taste. His reference to a vase and a statuette is equally applicable to his understanding of artistic form when he distinguishes between expedient machines and beautiful machines.

If we were to take this idea further, the result would be the division of life into the material and the spiritual, of art into pure and applied art.

This is the most dangerous of atavisms, since it represents the painstaking packaging of its old essence in external form. There is no true understanding of the machine when it affects you only by appealing to a new taste, only by the fact that it is beautiful.

The awarding of prizes to a machine for its beauty does not single out that machine from the rest for reasons of taste and aesthetics (although it could also be less expedient), but because it represents the simplest (and thus the most beautiful) solution to a specific complex problem. It is the quickest, most compact and most streamlined solution to a given problem.

In such a situation everything is based on the principle of constructiveness in the fullest sense of the word.

Yet another problem of modernity which many people tend to deal with very simply is facture.

In the same way the facture of today is not the same facture which people used to discuss.

Facture was extremely important and even decisive during that transitional period when artists were still fumbling intuitively toward a new construction of art. Here, in terms of the materialization of art, facture was initially a way out of a situation, but later it became an end in itself.

Facture as an end in itself is a negative phenomenon, in that it is art for art's sake. The first reliefs and spatial-constructive works were constructed on the basis of facture alone, and there was a moment when this new type of art, which presaged the creation of an entirely new form, became addicted, like Gogol's Pliushkin [a character in *Dead Souls*, pathological collector   ], to collecting bits and pieces of machines and combining them to make tasteful toys of a new type.

This moment succeeded in replacing the World of Art [Mir iskusstva] aesthetic with a new kind of spatial creativity.

Spatial art in the form it has assumed is definitely a healthy beginning. Apart from the element of representation it also contains the element of making, which is an extremely indicative characteristic.

1921-22

A General Theory of Constructivism

I. *Constructivism as ideology not as an artistic trend*

First of all, we should establish that Constructivism is a new ideology in that area of human activity which until now has been called art. It is not an artistic trend that we might present as a new treatment of artistic forms, one based on a fascination and enthusiasm for industrial machine-made forms.

Such an evaluation of Constructivism would not raise it above the level of an artistic trend.

But Constructivism is not an attempt to rework aesthetic taste into industrial taste. It is a movement against aesthetics as manifested in the various fields of human activity.

For the most part Constructivism is an inventive, creative activity, embracing all those fields which relate to the question of external form, and which implement the results of human ideas and their practical application through construction.

II. *Constructivism as the transformation of "artistic activity" into intellectual production*

Constructivism is the product of the revolutionary search for a new consciousness in art. After subjecting the creative process in the art of the recent past to critical analysis, we now discover that it contains new elements which have altered the entire character of artistic activity:

1. Construction of a painting based on technical necessity, rejecting the inner spiritual necessity.

2. Rejection of representation and contemplation in favor of activity and production.

The work of art (as idea + its materialization) is the result of man's perceptions and opinions about the external forms of the world, and the task of art is to formulate an ideal of beauty for a given epoch.

The perception of forms in the external world used to be refracted through man's center or "spiritual world," and thus bore traces of his religious and philosophical culture.

Hence the work of art attempted to solve the problems of the ideal and harmonious beauty posited by philosophical idealism, with its doubts as to the reality of the existing world and its opposing illusion of individual consciousness — "consciousness per se" — as something "objectively real."

Given its materialistic means of expression, the visual arts were the clearest and most complete expression of their time, and at the height of the idealistic world-view recorded and materialized idealistic dreams with extraordinary precision.

The ideal of external beauty is consistently harmonious and symmetrical, it has become axiomatic thanks to two thousand years of culture and has almost been transformed into something innate and instinctive.

Experimental cognition, as "active thought," as the action of the contemporary epoch (rather than contemplation), produces an analytical method in art that destroys the sacred value of the work as a unique object by laying bare its material foundations.

This rejection of representation has undermined the content of works of art created in the period of philosophical idealism.

New working principles have become a part of the painting — the development of craftsmanship and the solution of specific professional problems.

The formal approach is opposed to spirituality and ideas, and the work is transformed into an experiment, a form of laboratory work.

The work of art which functions as a source of entertainment and pleasure does not exist.

This revolutionary destructive activity, which strips art down to its basic elements, has shocked the consciousness of those who work in art: it has confronted them with the problem of construction as an expedient necessity. Based on the further principle of the expedient implementation of work, a new Constructivist ideology has been formulated.

The contemplative and representational activity of art is shifting to an active conscious action, and the concept of the spiritual nature of the artist's creative process is being destroyed.

Industry and technology are developing continuously. They astonish us at every turn with their unexpected external forms which find no corresponding echo in nature and run counter to it, making it impossible to establish an ideal of beauty for the modern epoch in external form. The realization of ideal beauty is thereby eliminated as a function of artistic activity, forcing the artist to move into industrial production in order to apply his objective knowledge of forms and constructions. For his activity that takes place outside real life (the reflection and elaboration of concrete forms) loses its meaning in the face of constant technological progress, which expects no formal canons from art.

For the first time in the entire history of art the problem of artistic form has been solved independently of our ideal conception of external beauty.

The atavism "beauty outside time and space" which we inherited from the idealistic world-view, with its unchanging aesthetic experience, has been destroyed by the analytic method. The result produces an action out of diverse elements and materials tasks, rather than the revelation of ideas according to a synthetic principle. Let us now systematize the factors that determine the Constructivist's new consciousness:

1. The development of industry and technology.
The concept of a harmonious beauty determined by nature is now redundant. Newly invented objects and apparatuses which, in their first principles, have no connection to natural forms, and which are aimed at overcoming nature, make it possible to construct a work of art whose artistic form is based on the concept of "artificiality."

The appearance in technology of contrasting and dissonant forms of construction rarely found in nature — for example, instances of achieving balance not just through the trivial principle of the pyramid, but, on the contrary, as in a crane where a triangle stands at an acute angle to the broader section above it. This has undermined conventional concepts about composition in art.

2. Materialism and experimental cognition.
Provides displacements in the very essence of the artist's activity, changing his view of creativity as contemplation and representation, and confronting him with the problem of dynamic conscious action. Creates further progress in the production process as the concretization of this action.

3. A series of discoveries in science and technology during the second half of the nineteenth century and early twentieth century has been recorded in art as the solution of formal problems dealing with technological necessity. The concepts of "craftsmanship," and "artificiality" arise as a second derivative of the work "art."

4. The social prerequisites that emphasize the abnormality of art's position as a specific function, the result of its isolation from the general tendency and development of social life, and its aestheticization (which, at best, is decorative).

All these factors have brought Constructivism to the point where the essence of artistic activity has changed fundamentally from spiritual representation to a conscious dynamic activity.

Being aware of this new activity is particularly important. Subconscious inspiration (a fortuitous phenomenon) is transformed into organized activity.

The intellect is our point of departure, taking the place of the "soul" of idealism.

From this it follows that, on the whole, Constructivism is also intellectual production (and not thought alone), incompatible with the spirituality of artistic activity.

III. *The rejection of art and the rupture between artistic culture and Constructivism*

Constructivism has analysed the "essence of artistic activity" and revealed the new factors mentioned above. Further analysis of the real concretization of these elements in art has made it clear that, though it has shrugged off the ways of religion and philosophy, art has been unable to give up aesthetics, which led it to maintain the painting's self-sufficient value. In other words, the analytical method was applied to art not as a significant modern principle in our thinking, but rather within the confines of the self-sufficient laws of art, i.e. as in the past the laws governing art persisted, separated from the rest of life.

As a self-sufficient value, a painting becomes the content of art, accountable to nothing. Religion and philosophy are replaced by pure aesthetics. How difficult it is for us to renounce the atavisms which we have accumulated thanks to our upbringing, and which we have inherited.

Religious sanctity is destroyed. A new aesthetic sanctity has appeared which can be defended only by reference to our forebears and by a few phrases about the value of art that resist analysis.

Even formal problems — the craft of painting — which were investigated at great length, did not enable us to understand the significance of all that had taken place in art or its goals.

Without Constructivism, therefore, the path of art, even in its formal achievements, contained hidden aesthetic traits of "art for art's sake" in the guise of craftsmanship for its own sake. The goal was not attained and the abandoned ideological content (which I regard as the real vitality of the art of the past) was covered over with an excessive degree of aesthetics.

This indicates the complexity of art's activity in modern culture.

Aesthetics, then, as a subordinate element, even in the analytical working method, leaves the fundamental characteristic of art unchanged, i.e. the realization of humanity's ideal by means of the illusory canvas of the painting.

Hence Constructivism moves towards the rejection of all art, questioning the specific need for art to create an international aesthetic.

But in the course of solving formal problems in art the term "technological necessity" is used figuratively, in reference to aesthetics. But Constructivism stresses a lack of continuity in artistic culture, excluding aesthetics as an unnecessary and forced form of stupefaction.

Similarly, the lack of continuity in artistic culture for Constructivist structures is rejected in view of its atavistic nature, which finds an aesthetic solution to formal problems.

IV. *A social theory of Constructivism*

Once purged of aesthetic, philosophical and religious excrescences, art leaves us its material foundations, which henceforth will be organized by intellectual production. The organizing principle is expedient Constructivism, in which technology and experimental thinking take the place of aesthetics.

In its specialized meaning, Constructivism consists of three effective acts: tectonics, construction, and facture.

Tectonics is adopted by the Constructivists to replace the idea of "style." The monumentality of a work of art created the concept of eternal beauty that existed outside time. The basic peculiarity of the modern epoch is temporality — transience.

In contrasting tectonics with "the monumental style of the past," Constructivism provides a definite ideological approach to working.

Every task can be carried out both monumentally and tectonically. Tectonics is a way of approaching the task as essentially a task, independent of the style of the epoch. Ideologically, tectonics cannot exist outside the experiment, that is, without construction and facture.

Tectonics is further distinguished from the monumental by its dynamic quality, which can change as soon as its environment, conditions or experiences.

As a principle, tectonics is the result of experience. In the present situation it is dictated by production, because material is being improved, experience and knowledge are increasing and providing new conditions and possibilities for formulating the task.

If we take into account all the qualities of the material, and approach the making of a thing organically, we will approach it tectonically. Hence the approach to a definition of tectonics as something organic and continuing.

Till now this continuing organicness did not exist, and though style was initially smelted tectonically to fit the demands of the epoch, it became an external form subject to the conventions of a given era and was subsequently understood in terms of aesthetic prettiness.

Hence stylistic form became the principle of the epoch, and the question was approached in reverse, i.e. from the principle to the experiment and the result.

Style understood as the organized form of an epoch — a form made canonical not by a principle but by its external manifestation — loses its meaning in the era of industrial culture. The ease with which external form is changed and produced decreases its value. Only the principle and the process are important, and the object is specifically intended to implement this.

The concept of a monumental style resulted from long hours of manual labor expended on each new form and object. Today, when the slogan of the epoch is "the temporary and the transient," there can no longer be a monumental style, i.e. the establishment of certain conventions of external form in a single complex, in the present day, when function, action, dynamics and tectonics are replacing the static object or element.

The conflict between the temporary and the monumental can be solved only by tectonics, i.e. the principle of ceaseless shift.

But the short-term significance of each new form contains a stimulus to futher expansion and evolution. Only a complete lack of understanding of the moment leads one to seek support in monumentality, where one is allowed to move right and left, but only on the same plane. If you move your foot forward, you declare yourself to be outside the process of continuity.

Lecture at INKhUK,
December 22, 1921

Dear Alexei, recent endeavors to move into production and material structures once again raise the question of facture. At one time facture was almost the exclusive province of painters. But later on, once it was realized that it contained aesthetic factors, it was, of course, rejected almost out of hand, since it had degenerated into the tasteful admiration of the way a work was painted.

Remember how almost everyone in the Constructivists' Group at INKhUK immediately started protesting when you read your paper on facture?

For everyone it was the material and its condition that had become important, not the working of the surface.

Understandably, the virtual rejection of depiction was radically reflected in facture, as in all the other elements of painting (and of art in general).

When art moved from a contemplative to an active condition the productive process, that is the concept of facture, changed with it. I consider facture to be a production process.

Until now, or more precisely until the first stages of our art (Impressionism), one could speak only of an artist's manner. This concept was extremely subjective and it often characterized the temperament of the painter. To a certain extent, manner was contained within, or rather confined to, several attendant material conditions and the general tendencies of the epoch toward this or that method of expression.

So the Dutch, in their small intimate genre pictures of rather dark and cosy rooms presented each color as a dense patch similar in effect to cloisonné enamel. Such dense paint application is typical of the entire generation of Dutch artists that preceded Rembrandt, and was directly influenced by the nature of the architecture that had created these dark rooms with few windows, in which the relatively translucent painting of, say, the French painter Watteau, would have been invisible.

In this case the general manner of painting was predetermined by a purely material factor, according to which the artists varied their own manner.

Furthermore, the more an artist was proccupied with transitory elements (emotion, literariness, representation and so on) the less we find factural elements in his work.

Whereas if he proceeds from purely plastic motifs while painting, he expresses a more pronounced facture which disguises his manner.

Take Leonardo and Rembrandt, for example. The latter is more material and plastic, and the surface of his paintings is worked with more variety. Leonardo moves the center of gravity to the emotional plane, which he expresses not through purely painterly means but through expressive means. One can only speak of facture in his work in terms of the patina applied by time. To consider the surface as painting is impossible; it just isn't there. . . .

Again, both our "Wanderers" and the Barbizon painters belong to the same general trend toward mundane realistic truth. But the Wanderers were gripped by literature and their works have no facture at all. The Barbizon painters' approach was more painterly, more professional, and the factural working of the surface is self-evident.

The painter who gradually adopts an increasingly formalist position moves first of all from the manner of painting to elaborate the plane, and then goes on to working up the state of the material.

Note that the transitional, experimental phase is richest in the variety of factural material.

Beginning with Cézanne right up to Constructivism, facture has been interpreted in an astonishing variety of ways, often entirely abstractly (as with Shevchenko and Grishchenko). So there is no single definition of facture. Except it seems that in the past, or in 1919, in most cases it began to be interpreted as an elaboration of the surface. Almost immediately this entire concept of facture was overturned by the sudden realization that this elaboration of the surface lacked a sense of expediency, whether it was organized as a purely aesthetic sign, or took the place of color as in Tatlin's work.

Interestingly, the usual MANNER of painting vanished when a painter began to phase his development, i.e. when he began to find solutions to formal and material problems.

Take Malevich's or Rozanova's Cubist and Suprematist periods. In the former they elaborate and finish the surface, in the latter it is simply colors, because color will not tolerate elaboration, if the goal is to demonstrate its strength rather than its quality. In other words, there are no longer specific manners peculiar to different periods.

In Rodchenko's work we see another interesting evolution of facture. In his non-objective paintings his facture stands out — terribly sharply — as one of the main elements whereby he reveals this or that quality of color — its weight, lightness, density and so on. Thereafter, facture appears as an expedient condition of the paint (meaning the material) for the problem in hand. Take a look at the painting you have hanging at your place, where facture is actually no longer present in its painterly concept as a way of extending the possibilities of color, but proceeds directly from the productional process of elaborating the state of the pigment (in this case its thinned-down state.)

The black and red lines have to be drawn with a ruler and for this to work the normal consistency of the paint must be thinned.

But the shininess of the thin paint which you see there has nothing in common with the flickering of old glazes, just as the bulge of the colored line has nothing to do with the peaks of the Cézannists.

Let me try to briefly sketch the historical evolution of facture:

1. MANNER (representational facture)
   Underpainting
   Impasto
   Glazes
   Rubbing

Impasto	Evolved not consciously in
Glazes	response to the material, but
Rubbing	from the drive to depiction

2. PAINTERLY FACTURE
Pressing through (alluding to density)

Layering of pigment (bumpy surface) — From the search for TONE in painting

Fortuituous painting effects, drips

Loading (paint thickly applied, mixing directly on the canvas)

3. WORKING THE SURFACE
(devised so as to extend the possibilities of color)
Adding sand, glass, sawdust etc. to the pigment
Applying foreign materials (pieces of paper)
Paste-ons (paper, bark etc.)
Facture created by stencil coloring
Working up materials (wood, iron, etc.) to simulate the old, "good quality" original.
Imitation

4. MECHANIZED FACTURES
a) use of instruments
blunter
applying paint with a spray-gun
roller and press
matte (mechanically even)
b) changing the condition of material
thinning for work with a a drawing-pen and ruler
shine — enamel-based paint

5. FACTURE AS WORKING UP THE CONDITION OF THE MATERIAL IN CONSTRUCTIVISM

Now I ought to go back and track down all the definitions of facture, as they have existed ever since this concept first appeared in art, and then look at facture in sculpture, architecture and the graphic arts.

I have deliberately not included Markov's definition of facture as "noise," since I don't consider it to be materialistic.

For now I still haven't touched on my own materials on facture, since they belong to the realm of a professional understanding of facture and complicate the question too much. I think it will later become clear whether I need them or not.

Now you're probably irritated by the "expansiveness" of this letter, but it's almost hopeless, I just can't write concisely.

I suppose I should work out a writing plan, or else I'm afraid this will be a disorderly correspondence.

Give it some thought . . . for the time being I haven't come up with anything.

Moscow
January 22, 1922

The move by the group of leftist artists away from easel painting into production has required them to make radical changes in their methods of artistic labor. This is especially true of the precise mechanical and documentary means of mastering "representation." As a result they are now obliged to adopt photography as a unique method for expressing reality.

More than any other, the field of polygraphy entails the re-presentation of phenomena found in the external world and confronts the artist with the formidable task of communicating these phenomena.

The journal, the newspaper, the book illustration, the poster, all these types of advertisement have confronted the production artist with the problem of making a documentary record of an object. The approximate, artistic drawing can no longer deal with the difficulties of objective documentation. The complex mechanism and external form of things of our industrial culture have forced the Productionist-Constructivist to abandon the hand-made methods of drawing objects in favor of the photograph.

Out of this the photomontage was born, i.e. the mounting and combining of select elements from separate photographs. In Russia the first photomontages were produced by the Constructivist Rodchenko in 1922 as illustrations to Ivan Aksenov's book *The Pillars of Hercules* [Gerkulesovye stolpy]. The book was never published, but Rodchenko's photomontages were reproduced in the journal *Kino-fot* (no. 1, 1922) as a new method of illustration.

The demand for a documentary approach is typical of our age and is not, as some people think, merely confined to the field of advertising. We are now seeing that even in literature, photomontage has earned the right of citizenship: the first major work to earn this honor in the illustrating of books, covers, and posters was Maiakovsky's book with photomontages by Rodchenko.

From that time on the photomontage has become extremely widespread throughout the periodical printing business, in agitational literature, and in advertising. It is a new form that has replaced drawings. Thanks to its enormous possibilities, this method is becoming so popular and indispensable that it is also reaching workers' clubs and teaching institutions, where the incorporation of photomontage into wall newspapers can easily accommodate the topics of the day. Photomontage is especially suitable for helping with campaigns, festivities, and extra-special events, and for organizing study areas and reading rooms.

All the Soviet publishing houses ("Gosizdat," "Molodaia gvardiia," "Transpechat," "Komakademiia," "Teakinopech-at," "Gosudarstvennoie voennoe isdatelstvo," "Krasnaia nov") have adopted photomontage as one of the most acceptable methods for designing covers and posters, as well as movie-posters. The years 1924, 1925, and 1926 were years of widespread enthusiasm for photomontage in the Soviet press.

In the brief period of its existence and dissemination, photomontage has already passed through a number of developmental stages. Characteristic of the first period was the combination of a large number of photos into a single general composition by cutting out separate photo-images. What linked them together were the contrasting sizes of the photos and to a lesser extent their graphic planes. This type of montage could be described as planar mounting on the white field of the paper.

Subsequently the idea of the photograph as such was affirmed: the print also became increasingly important in its own right. A major work from this period that should be mentioned is *The History of the VKP (b)*, published by Komakademiia and the Museum of the Revolution in 1926. It took the form of posters with photomontages by Rodchenko, in which the photograph was no longer cut up and now had all the characteristics of an original document. In this case Rodchenko was faced with the task of taking the photographs himself, since a montage of someone else's photos no longer met his more exacting demands for new shots that corresponded to the task in hand. So he abandoned the artistic montage of cut-out photos for an independent recording of reality.

This was the path taken by the first photomontagist, Rodchenko, who since 1924 has been moving increasingly into camera work. Instead of a cut-out photomontage, his works contain independent photos mounted separately or in series, the point of departure always being the value of the photo itself: the photo, that is, is no longer raw material to be mounted or combined to form a certain illustrative composition, but is a finished, independent work. This further increases the documentary importance of the photograph. It acquires the signature of the time and place it was taken, but also raises a new problem — how to make a characteristic and perceptive representation of reality.

Recently we have observed that almost any artist concerned with polygraphic production has equipped himself with a camera, as the only method of recording and demonstrating our reality. This allows him to completely discard the hand-made method of drawing.

1928

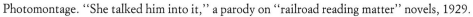

Photomontage. "She talked him into it," a parody on "railroad reading matter" novels, 1929.

The exhibition "Everyday Soviet Textiles" has confronted the public with the question of the artist's role in production, particularly in the textile industry. The following article was written by the artist V. F. Stepanova, who along with the late L. S. Popova, was one of the first artists to move into production at one of the Moscow textile factories.

Until the present, artists have worked in the textile industry along the lines of decoration and the application of decorative patterns to pre-existing fabrics. The artist has taken no part in either the application of new dyeing processes, in working out new fabric structures, or in inventing new materials for fabrics. Though he works in an industrialized factory he retains all the hallmarks of a handicraftsman. He has become the decorative executor of the so-called "demands of the market," which have evolved without any contribution from him. Therefore, the artist's importance to the textile industry is negligible, even compared to that of the artist-constructor in a car factory.

Textile production has preserved the artist in the swamp of petit-bourgeois taste by linking his work to so-called "fashion."

Ultimately the artist is transformed into a trade draftsman vulnerable to every vagary of the trade apparatus. The artist has no independence and has nothing with which to demonstrate the validity of his achievements, his aspirations, and his projects. The principle of expediency, which motivates design in every other sphere of industry, has no standing with him, and he has no incentive to develop that very field where, at first sight, it would seem that artistic design should reign supreme.

Costume design. Colored pencils on paper, 41 × 29.

The only correct approach would be for the artist to participate, at first, in clothing design. Out of this would develop his participation in the manufacture and dyeing of the fabric.

"Fashion" is directly affected by fabric designs — usually the cut of a garment presupposes existing types of fabrics and fabric designs — which means that printed fabric is subject to more frequent changes in pattern, whereas the facture of the fabric or the manner in which it is manufactured exerts a significantly greater influence on the cut of the garment and is more impervious to changes in fashion.

It is a mistake to think that fashion is an unnecessary appendage. In the final analysis, so-called "fashion" follows in the wake of rationalization, just as our way of life is also becoming gradually more rationalized.

In a planned Socialist economy fashion will depend, not on competition in the market, but on the improvement and rationalization of the garment and textile industries. The textile artist will then occupy an independent, responsible position both in the factory and in the trade and sales apparatus. We may predict that not a single production shop will be able to function without him, but he will have to make significant changes in the way he works. He will have to become more of an artist-technician, and his creative work will be rationalized along with the factory itself.

In the future we won't have stylish clothing that characterizes the life-style of society in every detail.

The decline of graphic design and ornamentation which we are now observing in many fields of art indicates that the fabric printing industry no longer has much of a future. The artist's whole attention should be focused on the processing and coloring of fabric, and on working out new fabric types.

Pattern can be of some importance in the details of a garment, where it will probably continue to be used for decoration. Like everything else pattern will be submitted to a standard and will ultimately be expressed through the structure of the fabric.

The principal task of the textile artist now is to coordinate his work on fabric design with the design of the garment, to refuse to design fabrics in the abstract for an unknown purpose, to eliminate all handcraft working methods, to introduce mechanical devices with the aim of geometricizing his working methods and, most important (and at the moment what is really lacking), to infiltrate the life of the consumer and find out what happens to his fabric after it is shipped from the factory.

The gulf that separates the fabric from the garment made out of it is becoming a great obstacle to improving the quality of our clothing production.

We can no longer speak of compiling a pattern. It is time to move from designing a garment to designing the structure of a fabric. This will immediately allow the textile industry to abandon the excessive assortment it now operates with, and will make it possible to really standardize and improve, at last, the quality of its production.

Vechernaia Moskva
1929

The State Publishing House of the Visual Arts proposed that we undertake a serious and responsible task: to provide an artistic representation of the First Cavalry Army, whose military activity was an unbroken chain of unsurpassed heroic exploits. Against the background of the Civil War and the sorry state of the country, we were to follow the glorious path of the First Cavalry, as it moved from the Southern Front in Poland on to the Wrangel Front.

We conceived the project as an artistic photo-documentary which would span the entire period of the Civil War, from 1918 to 1921.

There is no systematic history of the First Cavalry Army in books on the Civil War. We had to piece together the events from the memoirs of participants and from newspaper and magazine articles, and the material had to be gathered in fragments, laboriously and over a long period of time.

At the TsDKA [Central Club of the Red Army], the Museum of the Red Army, and in various libraries we came across scores of orders, pamphlets, and pages taken from the field notes of Voroshilov and Budenny and from contemporary newspapers. This material had to be brought to life in some way. One method we used in our work was to accompany the historical document with a photograph, a picture, or a poster. For example, on the page dealing with the end of Wrangel, we took the newspaper *Red Cavalryman*, the organ of the First Cavalry's political section, and underneath the announcement about the occupation of Simferopol, Feodosii, Sevastopol and Yalta, we mounted a painting by the artist Grekov.

Our work on the album was complicated by the fact that very few photographic materials had survived from the Civil War. The odds and ends received by the Central Photo and Film Archive and the Central House of the Red Army were incidental, and for the most part showed important personalities of the day. We took great pains to work up these shots. In one photo which recorded the taking of Rostov, we added clouds and extra ranks of Red Army men. This use of montage created a large artistically designed picture recording an important historical moment.

So that we could be sure we were accurately reconstructing the sequence of events, Izogiz organized meetings with members of Budenny's cavalry . . . where old-timers reminisced.

Our meeting with the commander of the First Cavalry, established on the Southern Front, S. M. Budenny, was of enormous benefit. Semion Mikhailovich had vivid stories to tell about many moments in the history of the First Cavalry, its moods, day to day episodes and individual heroic exploits.

To photograph some of these moments, we were sent on missions to the battle sites. There were two such expeditions: one to the area of the battles with Denikin, the other to the region where the battles with Poland occured. A series of dramatizations was staged and photographed at both sites — near Rostov, at Budenovskaia (formerly Platovskaia) Station, and in the Selsky neighborhood.

The material dealing with the exploits of the First Cavalry on the Polish front was presented as a photo-narrative told by a regimental commander to Red Army men about the glorious battles fought to consolidate the Soviet system in our country. Scarcely any photographic material has survived from this period of the Civil War, and only the dramatizations in which the warriors of the First Cavalry took part made it possible to fill in this gap.

To give the fullest possible picture of the Red Cavalry's military past, we incorporated paintings by well-known artists like Grekov and Avilov, and posters issued at both the battle sites and in Moscow, into the text. We got a lot of material from the "ROSTA Windows," among them the posters drawn by V. Maiakovsky ("Two-Faced Atlanta," . . . etc.).

The well-known Kukryniksy caricaturists were commissioned by Izogiz to make several drawings for the section of the album called "Those We Beat" (Denikin, Krasnov, Wrangel, Makhno, et al.). These drawings were completely original and had never been published.

The final pages of the album were filled with photos depicting the transition from the period of the Civil War to that of peaceful construction, together with shots of the cavalrymen of today. . . . The album throws into relief the role of "the Lugan metal-worker," Comrade Voroshilov, in the battle against the enemies of the Revolution, while comrade Budenny is shown as commander of the Red Cavalry.

The book concludes with a montage contrasting the old and the new cavalry, flanked by the portraits of Comrades Stalin and Voroshilov.

The photo-journalists' assignments were complex and difficult. They tackled the project with total dedication and demonstrated considerable creative initiative. Much effort was needed to provide high-quality material which would meet the requirements and plan of the book.

A few individual contributions were made by the photo-journalists Petrusov, Shagin, Moisei Nappelbaum, Dmitrii Debabov and Langman, although they did not constitute large portions of the album.

As a whole, the photos were inspected by the Peoples' Commissar of Defense, Comrade Voroshilov. Kliment Efremovich guided the compilers of the book with valuable and valid observations. For the most part Comrade Voroshilov approved the artists' work.

The album of forty printed pages has been submitted for printing, and the First Model Printing House is now working on it. The book will be printed in polychrome. Offset, mezzotint, phototypes and other printing techniques will be used.

The book will be released in time for the 19th Anniversary of the Great October Revolution.

The successful completion of our work on the album has inspired us to new labor. We have now embarked on the creation of the book *Twenty Years of RKKA* [Red Army Women Workers and Peasants].

Alexander Rodchenko
Varvara Stepanova
1936

Draft Syllabus for a Course in Artistic Composition in the Textile

1. Composition of designs of a preparatory nature for all sectors of the textile industry with a view to discovering the relations between principles of composition and color

a) composition of a design with planar forms
b) composition of a design with linear forms
c) composition of a design made up of planar and linear forms
d) design of a reproducible graphic pattern (of the grid type)
e) composition of a design with distinct and well-spaced structures
f) schematizing the use of a color for a monochromatic pattern; identical exercise for patterns with two or more colors
g) designing a combination of colors that completely alters the compositional character of a given pattern
h) reducing and/or multiplying the elements of a design to find the basic proportions of the forms of a given composition
i) designing a combination of colors according to the principle of chromatic complementarity in order to create the effect of a third color
j) design of a bichromatic pattern to create a polychrome effect
k) composition of a design that creates chromatic effects (iridescence for example)

The themes of the exercises in section 1 include designs for printed and woven fabrics as well as designs for the individual parts of a garment and finished articles.

2. Sample designs for the textile industry to be used in the production of finished articles

a) *in a single color*
Exercises: borders for bedcovers, towels, gloves, napkins
b) *in two colors*
Exercises: headscarves and handkerchiefs, socks for playing football (supports and knitted patterns), scarves, knitted caps, drapes, etc.
c) *in several colors*
Exercises: sports shirts, shawls, standards, knitted garments, awnings, rugs, etc.

3. Production and creativity in the textile industry

A. Composition of a design for a fabric for personal use
a) *light material*
    1. with a sample pattern
    2. choice of color for a fabric without sample pattern
Exercises: voile, printed cotton, woven cotton, light woollen cloth, realization of the different parts of a complete garment, linen, etc.
b) *heavy material*
    1. with a sample pattern
    2. choice of color for a fabric without sample pattern
    3. treatment of fabric (stretching)
    4. choice of a range of fabrics and their combination with different materials
Exercises: fabric for skirts, bedcovers, trousers, fabrics for heavy clothing

B. Composition of designs for fabrics of public use

Exercises: fabrics or sample patterns for furnishing, drapes, upholstery, linen for canteens and hotels

4. Designs for fabrics and garments

a) *work clothes*
Exercises: railway engineer, mechanic, workman, weaver, printer, switchboard operator, driver, agronomist, etc.
b) *protective clothing*
Exercises: medical staff, firemen, etc.
c) *sportswear*

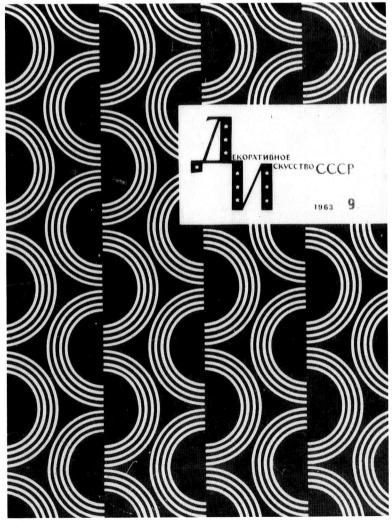

Cover for *Decorative Art of the USSR* [Dekorativnoe iskusstvo SSSR], no. 9, 1963. Based on the fabric design on p. 92.

Exercises: outfits for basketball, hockey and soccer teams, for gymnastic clubs, track suits for physical exercise and all other sports

d) *uniforms*

Exercises: staff of individual authorities, undertakings or the like (ticket collectors, clerical workers, Mosselprom personnel, etc.), children and teachers (orphanages, schools, colleges)

e) *clothing for daily use*

Exercises: clothes for holidays, festivites, public demonstrations and parades, lounge wear, multipurpose clothing, underwear, etc.

f) *theatrical costumes*

The graphic design of fabrics and outfits comprises: the outfit itself, shoes, hats, etc.

The choice of fabrics for the outfit is made on the basis of four patterns:

1. fabric with sample pattern
2. choice of colored fabrics
3. combination of solid color fabrics and patterned fabrics
4. combinations of different and special purpose materials: leather, oilcloth, woollen cloth, etc.

5. *Designs for emblems, standards and flags, decorations embroidered on costumes, details of clothing, window displays*

Exercises: standards and emblems for the "Dobrochim" (Voluntary Association for the Chemical Industry), the "Dobrolet" (Voluntary Association for the Aircraft Industry) and for radio hams, caps for postmen, insignia for army units, belts, collars, lapels, etc.

6. *Study of and research into the development and establishment of a modern style*

a) direct observation and sketches of the designs in vogue for fabrics produced by Soviet industry
b) study of the evolution of and changes in so-called "fashion" and related analysis
c) study of the current situation, with a view to devising methods that will demonstrate an awareness of the imperatives imposed on us by new social conditions

The syllabus refers to a course of four years duration; the first year does not cover the contents of section 3, on which work begins in the second year. The third year does not include section 1. Apart from the aforesaid differences, each year of the course includes exercises of increasing complexity and ever greater attention to detail.

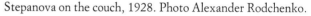

Stepanova on the couch, 1928. Photo Alexander Rodchenko.

Remembering Our Grandmother, Alexandra Ivanovna Stepanova

Our grandmother was born more than one hundred years ago (she was a contemporary of Lenin) in a Moscow barracks, since her father Ivan Vasiliev was serving a long, twenty-five year military service. When he had completed it and received the rank of non-commissioned officer, he decided to move with his wife and children to his native town of Kostroma. Grandmother grew up in Moscow and while still a little girl remembered the Iverskaia Chapel on Red Square, the haggling of the merchants and the pedlars' wares. . . .

Arriving in Kostroma the family (in addition to Grandmother there were three sons, Nikolai, Petr and Konstantin) moved into the basement of a brick house on a beautiful central street. The house is still standing to this day. Sometimes I walk past it and see that the basement windows have been sealed up tight. . . .

The retired officer's sons went to school, the oldest to the Technical School, the other two the gymnasium. Grandmother only finished elementary school, although with a Certificate of Honor. She was a very gifted girl and wanted to continue her studies and become a teacher, but the family lacked the means. Her mother (our great-grandmother) was a thin and furious redhead. Each day she did the rounds of the wealthy houses. She was a seamstress, and sewed linen from batiste and did satin-stitch embroidery. The retired officer, meanwhile, would go each day to his office, where he would write for pennies a piece Petitions to his Imperial Majesty — that is, the tsar. He had a most artistic hand! Then when he'd been paid he would of course get drunk and come home "on his eyebrows," as the common folk say. But always presents for the children — spice cakes, candies, sweets. And with strings of *baranki* [ring-shaped buns] hanging round his neck. And he died of what they used to call dropsy.

His family, a widow with four children, collected a tiny pension for him. My grandmother had to work. She accompanied her mother and helped her sew and embroider.

At the age of sixteen she was married off to our grandfather, Fedor Ivanovich Stepanov. He too was the son of a retired soldier, and had little education, though by nature he was a gifted man. As a boy he had sung in the choir of the Trinity Cathedral in the Ipatiev Monastery. He had a wonderful voice, a baritone. Grandmother didn't marry grandfather for love. He was twelve years her senior and all his life until his dying day he loved and worshipped "Sashenka." And always, as a young man and an old one, he would sing her his favorite song: "Just wait, wait a minute, my beauty." They were happy!

The wedding was a modest one. Grandfather worked as a clerk at the wharves of the "Rus" shipping company, and then was offered a position in one of the cities on the Southern border, where the cities of Kaunas, Grodno and Vilnius now are. Grandfather and Grandmother set out. My grandfather sat the exam for the very lowest rank, an official of the fourteenth class, and despite his poor education at a parish school, he passed it. He was well-read and intelligent but had a fiery and hot-tempered nature. He was an excellent family man and he loved children. In Grodno, Zhorzhik and my mother were born, while Varya was born in Kaunas. Not having had an education herself, my grandmother vowed that all her children would receive a good one. All the children studied at a gymnasium, although financially this was by no means easy. My grandfather's pay was rather modest. To be able to feed her family, my grandmother learned Polish and could speak it fluently, since at the bazaar no one wanted to sell food to Russians. But Grandmother was a skillfull housekeeper. She sewed all the childrens' clothes and took in gymnasium students as lodgers, while Varya, being the eldest and already a student at the gymnasium, was a tutor. Varvara was an excellent student and it was at the gymnasium that her penchant for drawing, painting and modeling became apparent.

Grandmother told a story of how, one day, Varvara modeled a figure of her teacher out of wax. Its likeness to the original was striking and one of the women teachers asked to have it as a keepsake.

Varvara Fedorovna graduated from the gymnasium with the right to a gold medal, but the medal was expensive and they didn't buy it. Before the war our family had a five-volume set of Gogol's works, presented to Varvara Stepanova on her graduation. Before the First World War began in 1914, Stepanova went to study at the art school in Kazan.

I still have in my possession a diary of my mother's (Zina) in which she writes: "1913. I'm no longer studying at the gymnasium. The doctor has forbidden it, he says I'm chronically anaemic! I live in this boring provincial town and I'm bored." This provincial town was called Sokolka. Varvara would write letters to her sister Zina. From one of these letters it is clear that she had got married to Mitia Fedorov in Kazan. While a student at the Kazan Art School she lived in an apartment at the Fedorov's house. Mitia was an architect by profession. He is shown in a photograph alongside Varvara Stepanova and Grandmother, wearing a suit and hat. When the First World War began, Grandmother abandoned all their belongings and caught practically the last train back to Kostroma. Here they rented a small apartment in a wooden house, where I was born. My grandfather worked at the wharves, Zhorzhik and Zina attended the gymnasium.

Then the Revolution struck, and my mother joined the Bolsheviks, as Grandmother used to say. Zhorzhik fought in the Civil War in Budenny's First Cavalry Army. But one evening there was a knock at the door. Grandmother went downstairs with a lighted kerosene lamp and fainted. It was Zhorzhik. He was all torn up and had just escaped. He took a long time to recover, but even afterwards during the night he would mutter and sometimes cry out "Saddle the horses! The whites are attacking!"

In the city he organized a branch of Osoviakhim [Society for Assistance to the Defense and the Aviation and Chemical Construction of the USSR]. He married Niura Petrova and moved to Moscow at the invitation of a friend from the front.

At about the time I was born, my mother was already the secretary of agitational propaganda in the provincial committee of the Communist Party. But she had never been in good health and contracted tuberculosis. When I was just a year old I was left without parents. My mother had quarreled with my father for some reason (youth, most likely) and he left the city. My grandmother worked in the city Soviet as a technical secretary, and then before the war as a controller in the State Bank. My grandfather cooked dinner and raised me. In 1939 he died in my arms.

S. G. Stepanova

Varvara Fedorovna Stepanova was born in 1894 in Kaunas (Kovno). Her father was Fedor Ivanovich Stepanov (1862-1939), her mother Alexandra Ivanovna Stepanova, née Vasilieva (1874-1950). In Kovno Stepanova graduated with a gold medal from the gymnasium. She entered the Kazan Art School and studied there from 1910 to 1913. From 1913 on she started to work independently and to show her work at art exhibitions. At the Kazan Art School she met Alexander Rodchenko. Without graduating she left for Moscow.

1915-17: worked as a book-keeper in a metal goods factory, then as a secretary-typist. She studied painting in the studios of Youn and Leblanc.

1916: Stepanova and Rodchenko began living together in Moscow.

1917: began writing non-objective poetry, based on the expressive combination of sounds.

1918: produced a series of graphic poetry based on non-objective poems for the books *Rtny Khomle*, *Zigra ar*, and *Globolkim*.

1919: illustrated A. Kruchenykh's book *Gly-Gly*.

1919-1920: produced a series of conventionally figurative painted works (*One Figure*, *Five Figures*, *Chess Players*, *Musicians*, *Figure with a Trumpet*, *Male and Female Figure*) and a series of graphic works in tempera on the theme of the circus.

1919-20: worked as Assistant Director of the Art and Literature Section of IZO Narkompros.

1920-23: member of INKhUK.

1920-21: research secretary at INKhUK (for the Group for Objective Analysis and the Group of Constructivists).

1920-22: member of the Presidium of the IZO section of the Rabis Union [Union of Art Workers].

1920-21: made series of colored gouache drawings (*In the Artist's Studio*, *Transporting Pictures*, *Two Figures*, *Figure with a Trumpet*, and others.)

1922: collages for the journal *Kino-fot*. Decorations and costumes for the play *The Death of Tarelkin* in Meierkhold's theater. Series of linocuts on the subject of Charlie Chaplin.

1920-25: taught in the studio of the Krupskaia Academy for Communist Education.

1923-27: permanent staff-member of the journals *LEF* and *New LEF*. Article "On the Work of Constructivist Youth," published in *LEF*, no. 3, 1923. Projects for sports clothing, 1924-25. Professor at the textile division of VKhUTEMAS. Designed the performance *An Evening of the Book* at the Academy for Communist Education in 1925. Made advertising posters using texts by Maiakovsky.

1924-25: worked at the First Textile Printing Factory. Produced 150 fabric designs, 20 of which were put into production.

1925: took part in the "Exposition internationale des arts décoratifs et industriels" in Paris, exhibiting in the sections on "Theater," "The Art of Fabric," "The Book Industry," and "Graphics."

1926: worked in the film industry, designing sets and costumes for the film *Alienation*.

1926-32: involved in polygraphy; imposed and designed the journals *Sovetskoe kino*, *Krasnoe studenchestvo*, *Kniga i revoliutsiia*, *Sovremennaia arkhitektura*, *Za rubezhom*, *Borba klassov*, and *Smena*. Designed Maiakovsky's book *Groznyi* smekh [Menacing laughter] (Gosizdat) and *Ot Moskvy kup-echeskoi k Moskve sotsialisticheskoi* (Ogiz-Izogiz).

1933-34: worked as art editor for the Partizdat publishing house, designed the books *Zavety Lenina zhenshchinam vsego mira* [Lenin's behests to all the women of the world] and *Itogi pervoi piatiletki* [Results of the First Five-Year Plan].

1933: imposed and designed the newspaper *Kolkhoznaia mnogotirazhka* [The Kolkhoz Newspaper].

1934-38: collaborated with Rodchenko on the design of the photo-albums *15 let Sovetskogo kino*, *10 let Uzbekistana* (Izogiz), *Moskva rekonstruiruetsia* [Moscow under Reconstruction], *Pervaia konnaia* (Izogiz), *Sovetskaia aviatsiia* [Soviet Aviation] (Izogiz) and *Shestvie iunosti* [Procession of Youth] (in English, 1939).

1938-39: painted a series of landscapes in oil of Moscow and the area around Moscow.

1940: designed the single-volume publication *V. V. Maiakovsky*, and maps of Maiakovsky's trips to cities in the Soviet Union and abroad.

1938-40: designed the albums *Sovkhozy* [State Farms] (Selkhozgiz). During the Second World War Rodchenko and Stepanova were evacuated to Perm and Ocher in Molotov District, and worked in the Ocher Agit-poster studio (1941-42). Stepanova worked in a literary museum in Perm designing photo exhibits dedicated to the Second World War.

End 1942: Rodchenko and Stepanova returned to Moscow and their old apartment. 1943-45 they worked on the album *Ot Moskvy do Stalingrada* [From Moscow to Stalingrad] (not published) and the photo exhibit "Sovinformburo."

1945-46: worked as chief artist on the journal *Sovetskaia zhenshchina* [Soviet Woman].

1945-47: designed the albums *25 let Kazakhskoi SSR* [25 Years of the Kazakh SSR] (Kazogiz) and *5 let trudovykh reservov* [5 Years of Labour Reservists] (a one-off presentation album).

1947-55: Rodchenko and Stepanova worked together with their daughter Varvara Rochenko. Designed the albums *30 let Sovetskoi literatury* [Thirty years of Soviet Literature] (not published), *Muzei-biblioteka V. V. Maiakovskogo* [The Museum and Library of V. V. Maiakovsky] (not published), and *Sorgo-Dzhurgara* (presentation edition).

1947-1954: Rodchenko and Stepanova worked on a series of monographic posters for the publishing-house "Iskusstvo i Goskultprosvetizdat" (Maiakovsky, Leonardo da Vinci, Victor Hugo, Emile Zola, Nekrasov, Belinsky, etc.).

1948: worked on the albums *Tsentralnyi muzei V. I. Lenina* [The Central Museum of V. I. Lenin] and *Moskva* (not published).

1953: designed the album *Moskovksii metropoliten* [The Moscow Metro] (Izogiz).

1954-55: designed the album *300 let vossoedineniia Ukrainy s Rossiei* [Three Hundred Years of the Ukraine's Reunification with Russia], and *Belinskii* (Goskultprosvetizdat) with Nikolai Lavrentiev.

1957: designed Esther Shub's book *Krupnym planom* [In Close Up] (Iskusstvo, 1957) and Sergei Eisenshtein's *Risunki* [Drawings] (Iskusstvo, 1958) with Rodchenko.

Stepanova died May 20, 1958.

Agarykh, V. [Varvara Stepanova], *O vystavlennykh grafikakh. Bespredmetnoe tvorchestvo. Katalog desiatoi gosudarstvennoi vystavki. Bespredmetnoe tvorchestvo i suprematizm.* (Moscow, 1919), pp. 5-9

A. G. [Alexei Gan], "Front khudozhestvennogo truda. Konstruktivisty," *Ermitazh*, 13 (1922), pp. 1-2

Gan, Alexei, "V poriadke ideologicheskoi borby. 'Smert Tarelkina'," *Zrelishcha*, 16 (1922), pp. 10-42

Forreger, Nikolai, "Charli Chaplin," *Kino-fot*, 3 (1922), p. 3

Rodchenko, Alexander, "Sharlo," *Kino-fot*, 3 (1922), pp. 5-6

O. B. [Osip Brik], "V prozivodstvo!" *LEF*, 1 (1923), pp. 105-6

Varst [Stepanova], "Kostium segodniashnego dnia — prozodezhda," *LEF*, 2 (1923), pp. 65-68

Varst [Stepanova], "O rabotakh konstruktivistskoi molodezhi," *LEF*, 3 (1923), pp. 53-56

Vecher knigi (Moscow: Krasnaia nov, 1924)

Brik, O.M., "Ot kartiny k sitsu," *LEF*, 2/6 (1924), pp. 27-34

Stepanova, *Programma dlia tekstilnogo fakulteta VKhUTEMASa*, 1925 (ms. in the coll. of Varvara Rodchenko)

Varst [Stepanova], "Rabochii klub," *Sovremennaia arkhitektura*, 1 (1926), p. 36

Aksenov, I. A., "Prostranstvennyi konstruktivizm na stsene,"

Stepanova in Kazan, 1915.

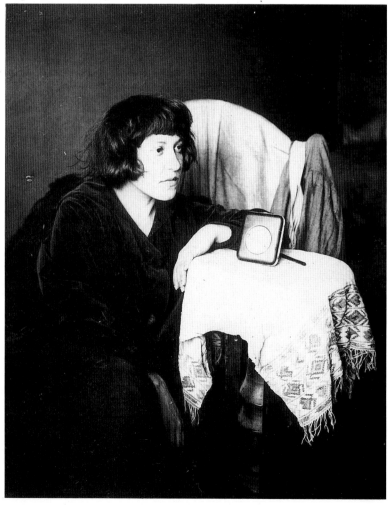

Teatralnyi Oktyabr. Sbornik 1. (L.-M., 1926), pp. 31-32

Aranovich, D., "Na pervoi sitstenabivnoi fabrike," *Vechernaia Moskva*, 242 (1926)

Stepanova, "Fotomontazh," 1929 (ms. in the coll. of Varvara Rodchenko)

Stepanova, "Ot kostiuma k risunku i tkani," *Vechernaia Moskva*, 49 (1929), p. 3

Matsa, I., *Sovetskoe iskusstvo za 15 let. Materialy i dokumentatsiia* (M.-L.: Ogiz-Izogiz, 1933), pp. 664 ff.

Shklovsky, Viktor, *O Maiakovskom* (Mosco: Sovetskii pisatel, 1940)

S.T. [S. Telingater], "Varvara Stepanova," *Poligraficheskoe proizvodstvo*, 3-4 (1946), pp. 20-21

Lapshin, V., "Zhizn polnaia poiskov," *Tvorchestvo*, 9 (1962), pp. 20-21

Abramova, A., "Odna iz pervykh," *Dekorativnoe iskusstvo SSSR*, 9 (1963), pp. 19-21

Abramova, A., "Nasledie VKhUTEMASa," *Dekorativnoe iskusstvo SSSR*, 4 (1964), pp. 8-12, ill. 13

Uvarova, I., "Veshchi tianut k sebe v noru . . .," *Dekorativnoe iskusstvo SSSR*, 9 (1968), pp. 29-32, ill. 15

Strakhova, V., "Sovremenno i ponyne," *Tvorchestvo*, 2 (1969), p. 24

Molok, Iu., "Nachala moskovskoi knigi. 20-e gody," *Iskusstvo knigi*, 7 (1971), pp. 35-62

Liakhov, V., *Sovetskii reklamnyi plakat* (Moscow: Sovetskii khudozhnik, 1972)

Strizhenova, T., *Iz istorii sovetskogo kostiuma* (Moscow: Sovetskii khudozhnik, 1972)

Stepanova Varvara Fedorovna. 1894-1958. Katalog. (Kostromskoe oblastnoe upravlenie kultury. Kostromskoi oblastnoi muzei izobrazitelnykh iskusstv, 1975)

Antonov, R., "K 80-letiiu Varvary Stepanovoi," *Dekorativnoe iskusstvo SSSR*, 7 (1975), pp. 44-45

Lavrentiev, Alexander, "Poligrafiia v chetyrekh izmereniiakh," *V mire knig*, 12 (1978), pp. 27-88

Lavrentiev, Alexander, "Poeziia graficheskogo dizaina v tvorchestve Varvary Stepanovoi," *Tekhnicheskaia estetika*, 12 (1978), pp. 22-26

Künstlerinnen der russischen Avantgarde 1910-1930 (Cologne: exhibition catalog, 1979)

Nakov, Andréi B., *Abstrait/Concret. Art Non-Objectif russe et polonais* (Paris: Editions de minuit, 1981)

Von der Malerei zum Design (Cologne: exhibition catalog, 1981)

Rudenstine, Angelica Zender (ed.), *Russian Avant-Garde Art. The George Costakis Collection* (London: Thames and Hudson, 1981)

Lavrentiev, Alexander, "Grafika visualnoi poezii v tvorchestve Varvary Stepanovoi," *Interpressgrafik* (Budapest), 1 (1982), pp. 46-51

Rodchenko, A. M., *Statii. Vospominaniia. Avtobiograficheskie zapiski. Pisma* (Moscow: Sovetskii khudozhnik, 1982)

Rodčenko/Stepanova (Perugia: exhibition catalog, 1984)

Lavrentiev, Alexander, "Tvorchestvo A. Rodchenko, V. Stepanovoi i ikh sovremennikov. Sovetskii graficheskii dizain 20-kh godov," *Interpressgrafik* (Budapest), 4 (1985), pp. 66-73

Elliott, David. *New Worlds. Russian Art and Society 1900-1937* (London: Thames and Hudson, 1986)

Gray, Camilla (ed. Marian Burleigh-Motley), *The Russian Experiment in Art 1863-1922*, revised (London: Thames and Hudson, 1986)

Khan-Magomedov, Selim O. (ed. Vieri Quilici), *Rodchenko. The Complete Work* (London: Thames and Hudson, 1986)

Anikst, Mikhail (ed.) and Chernevich, Elena, *Soviet Commercial Design of the Twenties* (London: Thames and Hudson, 1987)

Rodchenko and Stepanova, 1938.

Troepolskaia, Natalia, "Konstruktor Varst," *Rabotnitsa*, 11 (1987), pp. 37-39

Lavrentiev, Alexander, "Iskusstvo i revolutsiia," *Moskovskii khudozhnik*, 51 (1987), p. 4, ill. 1

Rudnitsky, Konstantin L., *Russian and Soviet Theatre. Tradition and the Avant-Garde* (London: Thames and Hudson, 1988)

Bowlt, John E. (ed. and trans.), *Russian Art of the Avant-Garde. Theory and Criticism 1902-1934*, revised (London: Thames and Hudson, 1988)